Navigating the Hidden Curriculum of Graduate School:
Thriving Inside and Outside of Academic Life

Navigating the Hidden Curriculum of Graduate School: Thriving Inside and Outside of Academic Life

E. Alana James, EdD
Published by *DoctoralNet Ltd*

For information:
DoctoralNet Ltd
8 Castlepark Village
Kinsale, Co Cork, Ireland
P17 KX76

alana@doctoralnet.com

Author Note

Because we have chosen to self-publish this volume, ongoing peer review is encouraged. This book was written for a primarily American context – therefore US English is the standard and I speak of graduate students even though in other parts of the world they would be postgraduate or early career researchers. I have tried to use dissertation and thesis interchangeably as in some parts of the world the dissertation is the Masters work and the Thesis for PhDs, even though the US uses the opposite designations.

Want to follow the links in this book but your university has not yet bought you a subscription to a pd.education site? Go to

https://pd.education/thrive.html

and register with your university email but choosing demo as the site. Then you can return to https://pd.education and choose demo at the bottom. This will give you full access to all the links in this book.

Abstract

Beginning with graduate school readiness and continuing through cognitive, pedagogical and metacognitive aspects of the graduate journey, this book is intended to help graduate students move through the rigors of the university with mor confidence. I try to explain the mysterious and give you options when you seem stuck. There is never one solution to complex problems and academic life presents everyone with both personal and professional challenges. The important lesson is that you are not alone. The goal is to move past challenges on to thriving.

Keywords: graduate work, Masters education, PhD, graduate school, professional development, cognitive development, socialization theory

What Others Are Saying About This Book

Voices from the Academy...

Oh my! Where were all these pearls of wisdom when I was going through my graduate programs? In these seven very reader-friendly chapters, Dr. James captures the essence and provides a rationale for what an individual will experience along the graduate student's life cycle. She succinctly articulates potential pitfalls and offers a variety of resources from self-assessments to instructional videos to guide the individual along the educational trajectory. The content of this book should be made mandatory for ALL graduate students to help them successfully navigate, and not only survive but thrive in their graduate experience.

JoAnn Canales, PhD
Senior Scholar-in-Residence Emerita
Council of Graduate Schools and
Founding Dean of the Graduate School (2013-2018)
Texas A&M University, Corpus Christi

*This book by Alana James makes an excellent rescue of graduate students who have dived into the "troubled waters" of graduate education. She provides advice, exercises in how to get support and negotiate our student life so you can see "light at the end of the tunnel." **It is the best field handbook for surviving and thriving in graduate school out there.***

David M. Boje, PhD
Professor Emeritus
University of New Mexico
Co-Author of How to Use Conversational Storytelling Interviews for Your Dissertation

Countless times during my 40 years in academic life I have counseled students about the nature of graduate programs. While students may be expert in their area of study, few understand the unique ins and outs of graduate school. It can be fabulous and also frustrating. Now, with Alana James' book, I have a reference to help them understand the educational process as situated within bureaucratic organizations.

More succinctly, as I have actually counseled many PhD students: No, you are not crazy. Yes, we all go through this. Don't take it personally, it is just how the system works. Patience and persistence win the game.

Grace Ann Rosile, PhD
Professor Emeritus
Author of Tribal Wisdom
Co-Author of How to us Conversational Storytelling Interviews for Your Dissertation

What Students or Early Career Researchers are Saying…

The life of a graduate student is often filled with real-life intricacies and complexities that none of the "How to write a dissertation" books tell you about. "Navigating the Hidden Curriculum of Graduate School: Thriving Inside and Outside of Academic Life" is a must have on any graduate student's bookshelf, as it clearly guides you on your academic path. Dr James shows an exceptional holistic insight into the challenges that a graduate student faces and offers practical solutions and advice. It is an indispensable part of my graduate journey.

Anelien Venter

Dear Alana,

Thank you for the opportunity to read and comment. What a wonderful book.

Thank you! Thank you! Thank you! I really cannot say it enough. The website pd.education by DoctoralNet has been a life saver over the years, literally a beacon of light that has guided me through both my undergraduate and post graduate studies. Your and Maria's videos and webinars have guided me through the nuances of postgraduate studies, and helped me become a better researcher. Having all this wisdom in book form is wonderful, and such a gift to future generations of students.

Erica Wynter

I have found Dr. James' wisdom about the graduate school experience and practical exercises personally invaluable. In this book, she imparts her decades worth of experience in academia to demystify the graduate school process. "Navigating the

Hidden Curriculum of Graduate School..." is full of suggestions and exercises to prevent or ameliorate some of the many unanticipated challenges that graduate students may face.

Erica Jablonski, Ph.D.

Granite State College

Dedication

To Masters and Doctoral students around the world, may this book make your journey easier. Don't give up on your dreams, they are worthy of your time and dedication. I am in awe of the collective ways in which you are an inspiration for the world. Specifically, for those who I have known through your attending professional development, this is your book as your input continues to enliven my life.

To Margie, without whom my life would not have blossomed, our partnership centers and guides everything. I am more grateful than words can convey.

And for Holly (pictured here) and pets everywhere who give us joy in hard times. Holly, as first a teenaged and then young adult cat, who met me every morning at 5am when I got up to write. You made me smile, offered solace, and were a pain–in–the–a.. when I needed distraction.

Thank you to the multiple students and peer reviewers who collaborated with me on the contents of this book. Gratitude to Adrienne Lew, Anelien Venter, Erica Jablonski, Laurice Howell, and Rebecca Hapes, all of whom were graduate students when this started in 2019 but many of whom have graduated, for being willing to pay it forward and help other students through sharing your experience and ideas. Your comments were provocative, and I am thankful you enjoyed the exercise.

Finally, without Prof Maria Sanchez Patiño, nothing that is DoctoralNet or MastersNet would exist in their current forms. Her webinars continue to draw hundreds each week to her particular way of breaking down the most subtle or complex into easy to understand steps. Thank you, Maria, for continuing as a friend, mentor, and clarifying voice which improves everything in the final output

Table of Contents

Author Note v

Abstract vi

What Others Are Saying About This Book vii

    Voices from the Academy... vii

    What Students or Early Career Researchers are Saying...
.... viii

Dedication.. xi

Introduction and Author's Note xvii

    The Format of What Follows.................................xviii

Chapter One Test Your Graduate School Readiness 1

    Knowing Your Personal Motivations to Help Keep Yourself
on Track 1

    Watch Out for the "Five Frustrations"...............................2

    Baseline Skills Needed..4

    Personal Growth and Identity 5

    Time Management...6

   7

Chapter Two Necessary Academic Skills 11

    Being Ready for Research.. 11

    Reading 12

    Academic Writing.. 16

    Argumentation 17

    Fallacies 21

    Research Design Logic 24

    Defending Your Ideas 28

    Bias 30

Chapter Three The Cognitive Skills You'll Need 33

    Intelligence 33

    Creativity 34

    Flexible Cognition 35

    Complex Problem Solving 37

    Critical Thinking 39

    Judgment and Decision-Making 41

Chapter Four   Three Key Ideas on Writing (and the Importance of Data) 43

    Voice 43

    Writing with Passion 44

    Data, Charting Your Future 48

Chapter Five Develop the Skills that Help You Thrive 51

    Thriving 51

    Your Mind Body Spirit Connection 52

    Metacognition 55

    Routines 58

    Discipline 62

    Building New Habits 64

    Resourcefulness 72

Chapter Six Transferrable Attitudinal Skills for Graduate School and Your Next Job 73

    Emotional Intelligence 74

    Negotiation 76

    Coordinating with Others 81

    People Management 84

    Service Orientation 90

    To Wrap this Up 92

Chapter Seven Troubled Waters in Graduate School? In an Ideal World... an Introduction 93

    Different Processes Around the World 94

    We're all People Here 96

    Motivation 100

    Re-engagement 102

    How to finish a big task when your life is already full..... 104

    To Consider as You Face Troubled Waters 106

Issues with Committees or Others You Depend On 106

    Academic Work Life is Not Easy 107

    Ambiguity 108

    Managing Expectations 109

    Too Much or Too Little Independence 110

    Calling for Help 112

    Timing Issues 113

    Additional Resources 113

Low Tide in Graduate Life 114

    In the Lab 114

    Food or Housing Insecurity 115

    Worry, Anxiety, and Imposter Syndrome 116

    Genetic Components of Stress 118

    Work-life Challenges 119

    Additional Resources 120

Your Rights: Legal and Ethical 121

    Ethical Standards for Academic Relationships with Students 122

    Legal Rights 123

In Conclusion 125

References 127

Index 131

The Hidden Curriculum of Graduate School: Thriving In and Out of Academia

Introduction and Author's Note

Since you've chosen to explore a book titled *Navigating the Hidden Curriculum of Graduate School,* I assume you are a Masters or Doctoral student, or someone interested in exploring those possibilities. Perhaps you are already enrolled and up against something that is slowing you down, causing frustration, or that you see as a potential problem going forward? The graduate school universe is vast and complex, and therefore it is only after years of working with hundreds of students that I feel qualified to tease out those complexities in a way that may be useful across the diversity of today's graduate population. Only you can tell me if I have been successful.

This book is built upon both the intimate experience of supervising students for universities, coaching troubled students through to completion and my company's research into what Masters and PhD students find helpful in terms of professional development. As many of you will know, pd.education by DoctoralNet is a set of academic and professional development services subscribed to by universities. Our mission is to help their graduate students have the support they need. On the research side, Susan Gardner (2009), identified five variables which cause graduate students to consider disengaging from their Masters or PhD programs. I have found them extremely helpful and call them "the five frustrations." They are ambiguity, work life balance, independence, skill development, and support. If you want to know more about where you stand in relation to others who have tested themselves on these variables you can go to:
https://www.surveymonkey.co.uk/r/5fs4hiddencbook

Most of the following sections contain an introduction that outlines the danger for students who don't have that skill or understanding, the basic information you need to move forward, an exercise of actions you can take to overcome those challenges and/or additional resources to consider for further, deeper investigation or study. Books are self-published for a reason. This one hoped to see publishing with a lower cost for students. Yet self-publishing is fraught with dangers of small and large editing mistakes. Please pass on your thoughts and stories, etc. to alana@doctoralnet.com - with the subject line Navigating the Hidden Curriculum - book notes. Through sharing you are helping future students, as this book continues to grow and evolve.

I'd like to finish with just a brief note about why I do this work. Through the hundreds and thousands of graduate students I have spoken with, and who have used our tools over the years, I understand graduate education can be a shining light of possibility in people's lives, their communities, and the world. People start graduate work for several reasons, but the thread that runs through most of you is self-development, having a dream, believing in something that is bigger and better than your current reality. Those are all fantastic reasons for humans to live and to grow. It is fulfilling to provide that support.

Over the years, as I have heard your frustrations with the graduate school process, I have tried to convey the multiple perspectives of student, professor, committee member and outside examiner. In doing so, I hope to demonstrate the good intentions that may belie actions that evoke your negative emotions and responses. While sometimes there can be situations that frustrate or hurt, those will diminish as you understand the underlying rationale behind such challenges. A change in perspective frequently allows you to maneuver through them with grace.

The Format of What Follows

Other students have worked with me on this book to keep it as concise as possible. I aim for each topic to include a short burst of ideas that will inspire and help you move forward, linking you to additional resources when you desire more in-depth investigation. It is my goal to have each section: a) tell a story or highlight the difficulty that this bracket of knowledge can overcome, b) include an overview of the basics of what it involves, c) include exercises, checklists, etc. that help you take action and d) give you additional resources. I delimit any intention of developing an exhaustive review on any one topic so that the book stays readable and accessible to anyone needing support.

In closing, I wish you only the best in your graduate work, and may you become a leader in your community and enjoy the enlarged capacity your new degree allows.

E. Alana James

E. Alana James, EdD
January 2021

Chapter One

Test Your Graduate School Readiness

The simile of Masters and Doctoral work as like climbing a mountain is more apt than like riding in a plane, both will get you to a destination but on a mountain, even with others around you, you are on your own, responsible for every move you make. Your previous positive educational experience may have led you to believe that if you just do the work in each class you'll move along to graduation. Is this you? If you believe that your university will provide you with everything you need to finish, then I recommend that you change your perspective and move to what I call "owning your experience." When you take 100% responsibility for every nuance of what happens to you and how you respond, your attitude will be more conducive to your success.

Knowing Your Personal Motivations to Help Keep Yourself on Track

I would encourage you to keep your questions in mind. Why are you either considering graduate school or enrolled? What do you hope to get out of it? How will this education advance your life? What personal values do you hold that will help you hold on when it gets tough? I admit I had only an intuition that I should start my doctoral work when I did, no clear picture of the why, yet my intuition was strong, and enough to keep me going. Today I live a life I could not have dreamed of. Pursuing graduate school got me started on the road to a fulfilling life. Whether you know what you want, or you don't, I advise you to keep your focus on the moments when you know that you are on the right path. They can bolster your strength when times get tough.

One secret to perseverance is to keep your eye on the future rather than only on the immediate situation at your college or university and in your extracurricular life. Without that future vision, much that goes on can be "a rabbit hole," as one of my online university students called it. A businessman, with a military background, he later said that he spent two years just figuring out how to voice his ideas in a way that others could understand (for more on this issue see the section on ambiguity).

Graduate school is frequently used to facilitate people changing from one adult context to another. Graduate work has many outcomes. It picks people up, moves you past your current realities, offers you new ideas and hones your skills.

The rest of this prelude lists some basic skills you will need, discusses the five frustrations you should watch out for, and suggests a strategy, proven by others to work, to help you keep on track throughout the graduate portion of your journey and beyond.

Watch Out for the "Five Frustrations"

Susan Gardner (2009) identified five variables likely to be part of the frustrations that prevent graduate students from completing their degrees. Since up to 50% of your cohort may not finish, it behooves everyone to be on the lookout for these frustrations and to pursue a solution before the frustration level causes you to consider quitting. The five are…

Ambiguity. You lose time and add pressure every time you act on a task when you do not really understand what you are doing. Humans communicate in a variety of ways. Culture has a role in how we perceive meaning. Taken together, it makes sense that the ways in which academic culture communicates may be wildly different than what you are used to. If something does not make sense, confuses or frustrates you, consider that it may be how the information is presented. Ambiguity often points out the distance in style between your current graduate role and your previous context.

To avoid these issues, don't act hastily. Keep asking questions. Search out answers from multiple people until you believe that you have clarity about what you are being asked to do, and the steps you must take to move forward. It is critical that at every stage of your graduate career you understand what is required of your work and how it will be evaluated.

Work-life balance. Worry and anxiety are symptomatic of poor work-life balance. Stress in any form is bad for our body, mind and spirit. Therefore, it makes sense to keep watch and plan breaks before you break down. Everyone leads a complex life with many roles and responsibilities. No graduate student feels as though they have enough time. You will experience stress. What you do not want to allow is for that stress to become anxiety or worse.

The first step is to consider how you will manage the stress you experience. Solutions include asking for help, building in support systems, taking time off. Be preventative, know the signs of stress or anxiety. Both are common challenges on campuses today so be honest with yourself and seek information, then help and guidance as needed.

Independence. Under what conditions do you thrive? If you are given too much or too little independence you may falter. Perhaps you like to work alone with little guidance, this is the system on which graduate curriculum is built. If on the other hand you like to work in teams with constant input from others, getting a PhD may be challenging. Continue to guide your options to ensure you have the type and amount of support that works for you.

You have options. Everyone is different, some feel comfortable with a neutral support person at their side, these do well with a coach. Others like to roam the net and thrive with the help of online forums. Many like to be part of a community and should start going to conferences in their field from the beginning.

Masters and Doctoral degrees help you stand as an individual within the topical environment of your field. This does not mean you have to be rugged, only that you need to be assured. Build the type of network of support that is best suited to you.

Skill development. Graduate work builds skills largely through a review process. You may not have anticipated the severity of critical feedback you will receive. Your culture may not have prepared you for an academic attack on ideas.

It is wise to grow tough skin when hearing others' critiques. Peer review is part of the academic world. The lesson is to consider the comment as an indication of where you can increase/improve your communication skills. One student recently shared that her supervisors' comment had set her back until she realized that if she wanted to be someone who understood the rigor of her field then she should use the criticism as a means to become more rigorous.

On the other hand, there is never a reason people should demean you, your intelligence or your background. Some may tell you criticism is not intended as a personal attack, but you may find yourself becoming defensive. If this becomes a pattern, consider reaching out to others, such as your Graduate School Dean to share the story and see if it falls within the boundaries of academic behavior.

Support. Humans need three kinds of support in differing measures depending on individual circumstances (mind, body and spirit). Universities are best at supporting our minds but may cause our bodies to break down through long hours of focused attention, and few students find them consistently supportive of their spirit.

You will therefore need outside positive influences to stay centered and happy while on the hard road of getting a graduate degree. If you come from a family or community where you are the first taking this route to advancement, then seek out more than your family and friends. When the going gets tough they may not be the cheerleaders you will need, not because they don't want to support you, but because the particular stress you are under is foreign to them. Likewise, just because your colleagues understand what you are going through, it does not mean they will know what kind of personal support you need. Learn to ask for what you need from those who can provide it.

Look at the experience of any of these five frustrations as a warning. Take action as soon as you feel like directions are ambiguous, you feel stressed, you don't seem to have the support you need or can't feel confident in what you are doing. The next section discusses strategies that will help you manage the complexities which bring about these challenges.

Want to test yourself? The following link will take you to a survey where you can test your relative level of frustration. If you find yourself ranking 3s or more, you should consider pursuing changes in that area. https://www.surveymonkey.co.uk/r/5fs4hiddencbook

Baseline Skills Needed

Some skills are useful from the very beginning of your Masters or Doctoral work. They include academic writing, critical thinking, argumentation, and a growth mindset. It is also useful to be able to negotiate. Learning these is iterative, more of a spiral than a straight uphill line. For myself, I thought I had any one of those skills well in hand, only to uncover further nuance and subtleties later. This pattern continues today even as I teach these skills, which leads me to recommend that, rather than feeling discouraged about your current level of skill, look at challenges as the lessons you came to graduate school to learn. Developing the growth mindset that allows this to be easy is covered in more detail in chapter two.

Other essential skills will also develop as you go through the process; how much of each may depend on your major. These include research design, thesis design, and academic voice. All have video links listed in the additional resource section.

Personal Growth and Identity

You might not have been aware that graduate school would require personal as well as academic and professional growth. Most students express a duality of experience, often flopping back and forth across a continuum from thriving to enduring. Those who thrive, who love it rather than endure it, are those who see the challenges as an invitation for personal growth. While some enter Masters or Doctoral work wanting to be a better thinker or to develop more understanding of the nature of measurement, the challenge to be able to overcome severe criticism and move on may not have been on their list. These are the personal lessons you take away and they will serve you well afterward if you embrace the full range of all the professional development opportunities you also have available. Getting into the habit of working on your personal growth from a mind/body/spirit perspective is a key graduate outcome.

When you graduate, you may come away with a new understanding of your identity. You will have uncovered deeper truths about yourself, have wrestled with some demons and come away successful. Already you have taken on a new role as you have moved back into "being a student." But you are not a student in the same sense as you once were. To gain independence you might start by redefining "being a student" to "being a self-sufficient and resourceful adult making your way through an academic environment."

5

In much the same way you would expect to behave when starting a new job, you should not leave any part of your skills at the door and revert to a passively accepting position. An as example, a mid-level manager had to be reminded that he frequently reported out to his superiors at work because those same skills deserted him with his principal investigator and his committee. As an undergraduate you may have looked to a teacher as having great control and guidance, here when you obtain your PhD, they are more like senior colleagues.

On the other end of the continuum, you also want to show respect for the knowledge and work professors had to go through to obtain all they have accomplished. In another case, the doctoral student failed because he could not listen to what his committee was telling him, he remained arrogant and did not respect them. This amounts to a failure to listen. The best middle ground is to give yourself permission to try out new strategies as you move towards success and to trust the guidance of your professors, at least until you find out what works best in your case.

Identity is a mix between how you see yourself, how you present to others, and how you believe you are perceived by them relative to the roles you play (*Stets and Burke 2014*). The process of growth through graduate life is iterative, changing, and fluid.

Embracing the opportunity to shed the parts that do not work and develop one or more new identities can make the graduate game more fun as you go along. I would suggest you consider what it means to you to master something or to be a Doctor? What do these roles or statuses entail for you? How will others treat you? What new levels of self-confidence, self-control, or skill do you expect to have at the outcome? Why not try these on for size now and act as though you have already achieved them? Attitudinal changes can be adopted and worked with, much as an actor takes on a new role.

Time Management

Time moves forward whether you have a strategy to support you, or not. Failure costs both time and self-regard. Avoid that loss by doing preparatory work before you are challenged. The three following exercises have proved to be instrumental in this regard. I recommend them for everyone.

Exercise one, the time management matrix. One of the best strategic discussions of time management is found in Covey (2016) The seven habits of highly effective people. He suggests we adjust our lives according to a 2X2 matrix as shown below (adjusted in this case to be graduate school specific). To work with this matrix, you should first consider what you value most. What is more important than finishing graduate school? Include those in the top row. What are your personal time wasters or behaviors that lack direct positive outcome? List those in the bottom row. This example is filled out with the nontraditional working PhD student parent in mind as they face many competing demands on their time.

The Time Management Matrix		
	Urgent	**Not Urgent**
Important	• Work project has a looming deadline • Bills need to be paid • Back to school night at children's school • Papers due in class • Family birthdays • Scheduled time with spouse and family • Tending to loved ones who may be ill • You may be ill	• Reading more literature for final research • Discussions with committee chair • Identifying summer or post-graduate employment • Attending relevant professional conferences • Participating in relevant professional associations • Submitting paper proposals to conferences/journals • Taking time out with loved ones, children and family members

The Time Management Matrix		
	Urgent	**Not Urgent**
Not Important	• Most Email • Facebook • Watching media entertainment	• Instagram • New movie trailers

Figure 1: Covey's time management matrix redone for graduate school

The point of Covey's matrix is that effective people strategically focus on the Important, Not Urgent box. This is where your work moves ahead. Fulfillment comes from that box as well. If all you do is chase the Urgent box your goals will suffer.

Exercise two, start with the end in mind. Just as you would not get on a plane without thinking about your destination and what clothes to pack for the trip, you should not follow the path of any curriculum only to stumble across its final requirements. How can you possibly chart how long something should take if you don't have a clear idea of what is required?

Will you have to do a thesis or dissertation before graduation? Perhaps you will need to have several published articles? Whatever the final task set by your program it is never too early to go to your library, to ProQuest or other repositories and pull-down models for what these final documents require.

Step one. Seek five examples of final documents in your degree area, some from your university, some from others. For a well-rounded search the five would include: 1) one in your topic area, 2) one that your supervisor worked on, or was from your department at your university, 3) one that investigates an area or uses a research design you can replicate, 4) one that has won awards in your field or is written by someone well known, and 5) one that is very well written, in a style you would like to emulate.

Step two. Separate and analyze the chapter headings of each thesis or dissertation, section by section. Critique the flow of ideas from your (the reader's) point of view.

For those not required to do a thesis or dissertation prior to graduation the same process holds true. Early on investigate final products from students who have graduated in your department and analyze them. How long are they? Did they require publication? Where are they on the continuum from essay to rigorous research? Does that vary? It is good strategy to chart a course based on your investigation.

Exercise three, backwards mapping. This exercise set the course that got me through to graduation from Teachers College, Columbia University, in three years. A professor walked us through the timetable, and I took it to heart. Your degree level and type determine the outcome, but the steps are the same.

Step one. Start a spreadsheet with three columns. Label the first date, the second what is due and the third, notes.

Step two. Fill in the date you want to graduate on the first column/row.

Steps three through chart completion. Fill in the rest of the boxes, moving down the rows/backwards in time. As an example, before you graduate you will need to be able to turn in a final copy of the thesis, or articles that constitute your final hurdle. This will be a second row with a date two to four weeks before graduation. Before that you will need to have them reviewed and approved. Before that you may need to defend (that takes some time to find and schedule the date). Etc. Talk to other students, gather insights and refine the time you think each will take. Each step gets its own date and description in the next row down. Quickly you will see how many steps you had not yet considered.

Final steps. Take your chart to an advisor or committee chair and show them your plan. Ask them to help you understand the final steps, and the timing required for each. Your question is how realistic is your plan? In what areas are their traps or systems of communication or processes at the university that will slow you down?

Additional Resources.

1. **Webinar on time management ala Covey:**
   https://pd.education/wellness-video-snippets/video/108-work-life-balance-in-grad-school.html
2. **Video: Beginning with the end in mind for Doctoral students:** https://pd.education/thesis-design-video-snippets/video/86-beginning-with-the-end-in-mind-4-doctoral-students.html
3. **Video: Beginning with the end in mind for Masters Students:** https://pd.education/thesis-design-video-snippets/video/85-begin-with-the-end-in-mind-for-masters.html
4. **Backwards mapping your graduate work and career:**
   https://pd.education/academic-writing-video-snippets/video/46-backwards-mapping-graduate-work-career.html
5. **The basics of research questions and methodology:**
   https://pd.education/research-design-video-snippets/video/26-the-basics-of-research-questions-and-methodology.html
6. **Thesis design video/ puzzling it out from lit to gaps to significance:** https://pd.education/academic-writing-video-snippets/video/1-puzzling-it-out-from-lit-to-gaps-to-significance.html
7. **Self-voice and academic voice, a video:**
   https://pd.education/academic-writing-video-snippets/video/58-self-voice-and-expert-voice-in-academic-writing.html

Chapter Two

Necessary Academic Skills

Academic work is a process or set of processes of mind. Training our mental processes takes time and is iterative. Three c's are important: critical, cognitive and conceptual. Criticality involves "a disposition for purposeful thinking and acting guided by criteria that are considered to be contextually appropriate and that are expected to result in positive outcomes related to the purpose" (https://www.yourdictionary.com/criticality). Cognitive process requires being conscious of your intellectual activity. It includes the ability to put together an argument, understand fallacies and biases, etc. and includes neuroscience. Conceptual has to do with the mind and the ability "to work with concepts involve a mental merging of philosophical ideas or imaginary outcomes" (https://www.yourdictionary.com/conceptual).

This chapter includes sections on being ready for research, reading, academic writing argumentation, fallacies, research design and bias. All are skills needed for graduate school and beyond. Each is followed by video resource links.

Being Ready for Research

Whether or not you are on an official research thesis or dissertation track, understanding the logic and pace of scientific research is important because these attitudes, and perspectives are the mental processes needed everywhere, but especially in a university environment. What does it mean to be ready for research? It involves what you know how to do, perspectives you need to take, and a practical understanding of how ideas go together.

Perspective dictates outcome and precedes skills. Science teaches us that none of our perceptions are irrefutable. Rather than seeing reality as a constant, scientific research has shown us that our understanding of the world is mutable, and any worldview may be called into question. As ideas change so do the institutions that guide our governments. As an example, just a few decades ago, our brain's cognitive ability was known to be fixed and any injury permanent. Less than three decades later we see brains are plastic and well able to overcome trauma. This new understanding led changes in entire educational systems, now seen as part of a process of lifelong learning and renewal.

Reading

To be ready for research, you need to be knowledgeable in your field and respect the ways in which your work builds on other people's. A first step is to go to the literature and do an in-depth study of both the foundational ideas and what is current in research and practice. It is best to start by looking into what scholarship is ongoing and to gather ideas from others.

Research training teaches us to measure, analyze, generate results and report findings. Based on the underlying assumption that the world is not stagnant, scientific work is also inherently innovative. Because fields evolve, by measuring current reality research builds a better model of the future. Academic developments are often incremental and time-consuming, but results are reliable. All of this adds up to an increased importance on the ability to read, comprehend and move past what is read to evolutionary ideas.

Consider your skill development in reading and comprehension iterative rather than conclusive. You will revisit ideas and processes you thought you knew well and then you will find they develop further. If you enjoy learning the graduate path lasts a lifetime.

Reading for output and designing your writing as you work. Solid skills in reading, comprehension, and complex organizational strategies precede research. A good place to start your professional development is to upgrade your reading and comprehension skills. As small children, before we learned to write, we learned to read, its foundational. Before we learned an action, we watched others do it. Books on writing uphold this same thread and extol that good writers are always good readers (*Zinsser, 2006, King, 2010*), therefore it is important you immerse yourself in reading the types of material you will write. Are journal articles in your future? Then read them. Likewise, you should read dissertations if you will be required to write one.

To see the advantage to reading widely, picture yourself as engaging in an academic conversation, perhaps one that takes place during a class discussion where your desired outcome is to be seen as intelligent. You have read a body of literature and have just made a point regarding the thoughts of an author. Someone else jumps into the conversation and goes further into the work of that author and the underlying premise on which the work is based. In the back of your mind you notice that, while you read the work, you did not see the intricacies this second person discussed. In order to give yourself a leading edge, you need to be able to see subtlety and put ideas into multiple contexts. These outcomes hinge on strong reading skills.

What does it mean to read academic literature well? The hidden curriculum for reading includes being able to read WHILE you are charting the literature in your mind and analyzing other connections. Otherwise you have to read or consider something several times to milk its linkages with other work. While reading and plotting in stages is a strategy that works, graduate life typically is short on time. The solution is to build a mind map in your head (or on your desktop if you prefer) as you read. Learn to sort, categorize and apply your reading to the rest of what you know as you read.

Academic reading also needs to be efficient because there will be more of it than you will be able to address properly. Be selective, make conscious choices about which material warrants your time. Developing the skill to investigate, read, sort and analyze quickly is necessary if you are to finish all the required texts in classwork, as well as to build a solid foundation of literature for your research.

The basics. Reading academic work is different than reading fiction. The reader of fiction suspends judgement and allows the author to take them on a journey of the author's design and choosing. This is opposite of academic reading where you should maintain your own sense of judgement throughout. "Do I need this?" "Is it useful to my work?" "If not useful now, is it interesting, and should I consider reading it later?" "How can I capture the main points so I can find them again when I synthesize?" Like a hunter, an academic captures idea and preserves them for another time.

It helps to be clear on the structure of writing. Titles inform the reader of the outcome of what the author or editors hoped to achieve from the material. In a book, chapter headings define the process the author used for sorting the ideas, giving you clues you can follow as well. Books come in two basic types. A single author controls the entire flow of content, making it easy to skip sections which do not apply to your work. Multiple authors contribute different chapters, each a stand-alone set of ideas. This means you will have to wade through extraneous content as you decide which key points are germane.

Three other parts of writing structure should help your analysis. First, headings guide the reader through central ideas. A quick overview of them make it easy for you to decide which sections are most relevant or pertinent to your work. Second, by skimming through introductions, summaries and conclusions you can make yes/no decisions about the time a piece of writing warrants. Third, paragraphs illuminate only a single point, making it easier to read rapidly by finding the key sentence and moving on to the next paragraph for the next point.

Know the outcome you are looking for before you pick up the text. Two examples illustrate this point. In the first, the writing is something assigned for a class. Your goal is to know it well enough that you can track the ideas or add to a conversation about it as that author comes up in the syllabus. It may or may not be useful to the final work in the class so when you first read it you do not know how important it will turn out to be. Therefore, your strategy is to overview the work, and summarize three main points. You can do this by first reading the introduction, then reading the conclusion or summary and perusing the headings to find where the summary points lie. Subtleties in the ideas are tracked by following headings around those points and delving in deeper as needed to clarify. Your first task is to identify what the author is saying and why they believe that to be true or what evidence they use to back up their argument. By the time you have gathered that information you should have an idea about how important this text is to your goals. When the ideas are compelling, new or refute another position, then go deeper and read until you understand the nuances involved.

In the second example, you are now in the library searching keywords, opening multiple documents, working on building a literature review for your own research. Two skills allow the first sort, during which you decide whether to set the work aside for deeper investigation, or to dump it and move on. They are skimming and scanning, and they work together.

Scan a title or introduction with openness to see what captures your attention. This is much like scanning an area in front of you while walking to see where you want to go next. Attention is a function of our reptilian brain and developed to keep us safe from attack by noticing anything different or dangerous. In this instance, safe is having captured the main ideas relevant to your study.

After spotting ideas that are different, you move to skimming, which entails reading the first or last sentence in each paragraph. Authors develop ideas in a consistent pattern to establish a pace in their work. Understand their pattern and you can skim his/her work more easily.

Exercise. The following three steps make up the basic pattern followed by researchers investigating a new train of thought. It is more efficient to repeat a step for multiple articles, rather than completing the entire process one at a time for every article you find.

- Enter potential keywords in the database and download or find those references whose titles seem promising.
- Scan the abstracts sorting your results again into those worthy of investigation or those you dump.
- Skim the introduction, conclusion or summary and if worthy, capture the reference in a spreadsheet or bibliographic software and make notes.

Video resources.

- **Using strategies to improve reading for Masters and Doctoral Students:** https://pd.education/criticality-video-snippets/video/224-using-strategies-to-improve-reading.html
- **Register reading:** https://pd.education/criticality-video-snippets/video/137-register-reading.html
- **Academic reading:** https://pd.education/criticality-video-snippets/video/243-academic-reading.html
- **Reflective reading with exercises. Part one:** https://pd.education/criticality-video-snippets/video/138-reflective-reading-with-exercises-part-one.html

- **Reflective reading with exercises. Part two:**
  https://pd.education/criticality-video-snippets/video/139-reflective-reading-with-exercises-part-two.html

Academic Writing

You are not ready for research until you can write about it in a style appropriate to your field. Because this is a topic that includes all the subtleties of language, this section gives you a only an overview of the basics. A video library is included in the additional resources at the end of the chapter for further investigation.

The basics. Thoughts have to progress in a logical manner and, while you may not always think of your work as building an argument, you want to funnel your reader through your ideas to the points you hope they take with you when done. I find the following diagram useful.

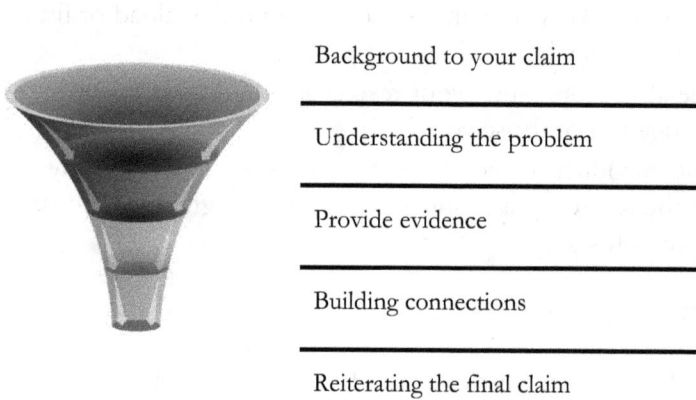

Background to your claim

Understanding the problem

Provide evidence

Building connections

Reiterating the final claim

Figure 2.1: Funnel your reader from wide ideas to your outcomes

If an argument, the top is the general claim, the next rung the evidence, then the warrant that helps the reader understand the relationship to the claim of the evidence and a summation that backs it up. If an essay, then the top is the background or context of the work, second are the specifics of the topic or the setup of the problem being discussed, then evidence or more detail that leads the reader to the outcomes you want them to take on.

You will notice that this funnel or argument format is mirrored in all writing through chapter titles (broad ideas), heading level one (the major steps that guide the reader through the content), subheadings two through four smaller steps and the paragraphs under each illuminate one logical point each. In a journal the authors follow the same steps with background, literature, methodology, results and findings.

A frequent mistake that causes readability breakdown are paragraphs that do too much and cram two or more points together. This enhances the potential of your readers becoming confused or, at the least, not absorbing your ideas. Since your readership will scan your work, make each step clear.

Video resources.

- **Know your focus before you begin to write:** https://pd.education/thesis-design-video-snippets/video/183-whether-you-call-it-a-dissertation-or-a-thesis-you-should-know-what-it-is-before-you-start.html
- **5 minutes on using MS Word for academic writing: Day 8 of the writing challenge** https://pd.education/academic-writing-video-snippets/video/186-5-minutes-on-using-ms-word-for-academic-writing-day-8-of-the-writing-challenge.html

Argumentation

The ability to form and dissect an argument is fundamental to academic life, yet it may not be covered in your coursework. Consider the story of Alice (not her real name) who was going ahead to the best of her ability through developing a proposal. She worked hard to follow all the content rules, clicking (or checking) all the boxes to meet the needs of what should be in each section. Imagine her dismay when her supervisor read her proposal and returned it with a cryptic note that she had to build an argument. What was missing?

You can have all the pieces and still miss the point. If your professor is not conscious of all the parts of argument, they may not recognize or be able to articulate the problem, yet their review will tell you they are not convinced. This results in less than satisfactory comments as you may not know what to do next.

An argument in a proposal lays out the reason the work is significant, gives evidence in literature for its importance and the gap it will fill all the while convincing the reader the methodology will lead to evidence that will fill that gap. At the end, your results must show that you have done that and that your findings fill the gaps in the literature that your work uncovered. All documents are more readable, logical, and convincing when you understand the basics of an argument.

You must go beyond that and make your work compelling. What makes the standard argument (laid out above) a compelling argument, is the addition of intrigue. Why is the problem you are addressing important? What have other people done before and how has their work failed to make the one difference yours will make? What remains unknown? To hold intrigue your reader needs to feel the gap as well as see it. Those are the problems that stick in our head and we wonder about them. That is the sweet spot you are aiming for.

The basics. Building a solid yet compelling argument entails: a) clarifying what is intriguing about the problem you are trying to solve and how the solution will be significant, and b) tying your claim of significance to evidence through data and/or research literature and then c) backing it up either through logic and/or methods to convince someone else of the validity of your ideas (your warrant).

Let's look at those steps again using the example of the problem that not every PhD student successfully finishes their dissertation or thesis.

1. First, you make the claim obvious. You do this through explaining the background or context of your ideas or study. In our example, even though there are many reasons doctoral students don't complete their degree, one of the significant ones has to do with not managing the independent work required in the face of the complexities of the rest of their lives, making finding the right resources for help difficult. What is intriguing is how to pull out the significant threads of the overarching issues from the specifics of student behavior. In other words, while we can measure what went wrong in one student's case, how can we extrapolate to changes in practice that should positively affect a larger population?

2. Second, you point out data (evidence) that agree with your claim. This can be others' research, philosophical or theoretical ideas,

18

or a lack of either which calls for a requirement to study further. In our example there are literally thousands of dissertations, articles, etc. that measure PhD student disengagement in a variety of means. These would have to be sorted into themes. What none of them have done, however, is to draw on wide enough samples of students (thousands) who use the same tools or to tie the use of those tools to student outcomes.

3. Third, you need to show the logical correlation between your evidence and your claim (this is the warrant). Warrants may be the way in which your ideas tie known circumstances or data together. In research it is how your methods address the requirements of the study, and, later, how your results lead to your findings that tie back to your claim. In our example, the warrant changes if the writing is for the proposal or from the final research findings at the end. For the proposal the warrant includes that since we can see that even though PhD disengagement has been widely studied, no one has used a significant or cross campus population to do so, therefore the ability to use that broad a population should elicit results that will make a difference to education as a whole. Once data is in then the warrant narrows the literature to focus on only the themes in which there were interesting findings. The warrant becomes a discussion of those findings and how they advance the field in that area.

4. Finally, you conclude making it obvious that because the reader can see this evidence, the warrant that those data/ideas build to the claim becomes obvious and therefore the claim is satisfied. Now that we know how a large number of students respond to the tools or supports that we were testing, we can convince the reader that these results are intriguing and should be implemented across the wider educational space.

How much you need to back up your claim will depend on your particular discipline or methodological context. If you are in a class and writing a paper then your claim is the idea which you lay down in your opening paragraph after which you take your reader through the evidence (often derived from the readings required). The skill you need to develop will be your ability to build a strong warrant between evidence and claim. You conclude with the outcome you want your reader to take away.

For a graduate or post-graduate research process, such as a prospectus, proposal, final dissertation or thesis, the work has many more parts but follows the same logic. Your claim is that your research is necessary, intriguing and significant and that you have the pathway that is most efficient to successfully address that need. You make the claim in your first sections as you overview the full argument. The literature review is your report of the prevailing evidence and you are required to point out counter arguments and gaps in the research just as later you must point out data that does not completely agree with your findings. Your theoretical or conceptual framework establish the first part of your warrant, giving your reader the tools they need to follow the path of your logic. Your methods section is a different warrant because it ties the need for further evidence with indications you have the skill and understanding to complete the research task. With all these elements you should be able to conclude that: a) there is a gap in the literature of your field that your data collection and analysis will fill using the methods you have chosen, b) the gap is important enough (significant to the field) and therefore justifies the work, and that c) you should move forward along your thesis or dissertation pathway. After data collection and analysis, you claim you have filled the gaps and have significant findings. You conclude that your findings build on previous research and that the data and analysis of this study prove your claim (that your work is significant).

This can be subtle. How to build arguments and what they entail have been the work of philosophers and academics for centuries. If you want to delve into these you can research Toulmin, Rogerian, and Aristotelian argumentation.

Checklist. Use the following checklist to ensure you have what you need to build an argument in your next work. You...

- Have a claim that you want to make on a subject that is intriguing.
- Have what you consider a sufficient amount of background evidence, whether data that show the difficulty your research/ideas will address or literature pointing to a gap that your research/ideas will fill.
- Write these ideas succinctly into the follow four sentence stems:
  - I claim...

- The evidence that supports this claim includes...
- These support my claim because...
- (For a prospectus and proposal) The methods I propose to use to research deeper into this topic involve.... (type of test, performed on, or in a certain way)
- Following this logic, the readers should see...
- Understand the format needed to build an argument, given the requirements of the writing in which you are engaged.

Video resources.

1. **Argumentation in Academic Papers: A Need** by Prof Maria Sanchez Patiño - https://pd.education/argumentation-video-snippets/video/10-argumentation-in-academic-papers-a-need.html
2. **What is argumentation and why is it so important? Slides** - https://pd.education/file-downloads/argumentation/434-what-is-argumentation-and-why-is-it-so-important-slides-20191510.html

Fallacies

A fallacy is an invalid argument built upon deceptive reasoning, something you want to avoid. Your argument may appear reasonable until you follow the threads and find yourself in a place where the warrant does not match the evidence and will not support the claim. Fallacies are tricky because they are hard to spot.

Universities typically spend little time talking about the mistakes people make when building their arguments. We say that the argument was fallacious when it falls in one of these types of mistakes. Being able to spot them helps you avoid being convinced by something or someone not worthy of support.

The basics. At a basic level, there are three types of fallacies, some done consciously and with intent and others caused by misunderstanding. The three types are: misdirection or equivocation, non sequiturs, and confusion with sourcing. There may be fallacious patterns in either the argument or a counter argument posed against it.

Misdirection or equivocation works on the same principle as the street game with something under one of three cups and the shyster moving the cups to see if you can follow his/her movements. These fallacies focus your attention by employing either a poor definition or a wrong premise. Either way your attention is pointed towards ideas that actually don't follow the logical pattern. Misdirection builds a false argument that has no warrant between evidence and claim. This is the most likely to be done with intent.

Non sequitur in Latin means "does not follow." Here A+B leads not to C but to D, E or F. The logical chain has flaws which you must pick out to refute the claim. Frequently employed during a counter argument, these may take the form of personal attacks. For instance, "How could you believe him? He is an idiot." You might also see someone discounting a claim by changing the focus away from the logic of the argument to the characteristics of the context. Irrelevant issues may also be introduced, as in politics or journalism were ideas are introduced to create an emotional reaction and therefore throw the logic off base.

Confusions with source make assumptions that are not true. The history of science is one of research overcoming fallacies that were confusions with source. The world is not flat, man can fly, and our genetic makeup will change over a lifetime. All of these previously thought to be untrue. Racism is a genetic fallacy that is a confusion with source, adhering to the belief we can know something specific about an individual based on a classification.

How can you avoid fallacy when arguing that your research topic is significant? First, are you aware of the ways in which your personal bias and worldview guides this choice? Will skeptics find this potential topic well-grounded in data and intriguing? Would your topic be compelling to most people or a few? Early career researchers have been known to explode their worldview and write about a small issue as though it had great meaning.

Be suspicious when you find yourself backing up an argument with "research has found…". Within in any field of study there are arguments about what is true. Research seldom "says" or "proves" or "finds" one thing, (not to mention research doesn't "say" anything at all as these words are anthropomorphic).

When critiquing your own work, of course, you'll avoid a fallacy caused by the argument being based on false data, but you still may fall into one that is really wishful thinking. Common fallacies include arguments based on too small a sample, where extrapolation to the wider population seems weak. You might follow a logical progression but end up in a trap or dead end. Be skeptical about your own arguments and see if you can find their weakness. For instance, "if-then" types of logic may have one or more of the common fallacious traps within them. Do not assume that if just because A and B are correlated in one instance that they have a relationship that will necessarily be true in other contexts. Always challenge any argument that leads to a prediction about the future. Improvements in machine learning algorithmic or genomic prediction accuracy continue as newer forms of measurement evolve.

It takes practice to challenge those arguments that seemingly have strong evidence but that prove causality. Scientific research has shown that, due to complexity of influence, causality is an almost impossible argument. Look for places where the warrant tying the evidence to the claim do not stack up.

When it comes to building your own arguments, write with a conscious effort to unpack your own bias. When you build an argument look for counter evidence and include it. Are you over tipping the true importance of that evidence? Trying to make it bigger than it warrants in order to advance your case? Are you trying to sell your reader on your ideas rather than laying down evidence in an unbiased manner? As you become as strong police of your own tendency towards fallacy you will see it more in others. Experienced researchers are skeptical of both evidence and claim.

Exercise. One way to learn more about fallacy is to build fallacious statements. Start with either an argument in your field or one in the current political environment, or a common belief about how people "should" behave. Work out the claim, the evidence and the warrant. Then go through the list below and make it, or its counter argument, fallacious in the following ways.

1. An ad hominem fallacy – attack a person who would believe the counter argument rather than the argument itself.

2. A tu quoque fallacy – point out how the people who believe the argument you want to counter take actions that invalidate their stance.
3. A red herring. Introduce an irrelevant aside to the argument that can be refuted easily, making the entire argument seem weak.
4. Appeal to ignorance. Build up any lack of evidence as a claim of disproof or proof. Just because we cannot see X means… or doesn't mean…
5. Your argument as an ethical slippery slope. Well if you believe X does that mean you also believe Y? If this, why not ….?
6. A straw man. Construct a fallacious warrant based on the same evidence but one which has flaws, like the red herring, when you disprove the straw man you undermine the original argument.
7. A counter argument based on the focus of one definition within the evidence or warrant. This redirects the focus of the conversation to that one piece rather than the whole. This happens in scientific communities where the methods used in the research overtakes the evidence derived from it.
8. A circular argument. This is where your evidence and your warrant just reshape your claim, nothing new was added.

Video resources.

- **Fallacies a path to failure:** https://pd.education/academic-writing-video-snippets/video/5-fallacies-a-path-to-failure-part-i.html

Research Design Logic

The student experience of research design matures through the Masters and Doctorate levels. It starts with the library as you search out literature and proceeds up to a formal document, possibly hundreds of pages in length. A research design always includes what you are studying and why it is important, the literature on which it is based, what questions you are asking, of whom or under what conditions, and in what manner. The answers to those questions need to lead the reader back to the importance of the study, the argument that you are making of its significance. The following simple diagram may help you lay out all these parts.

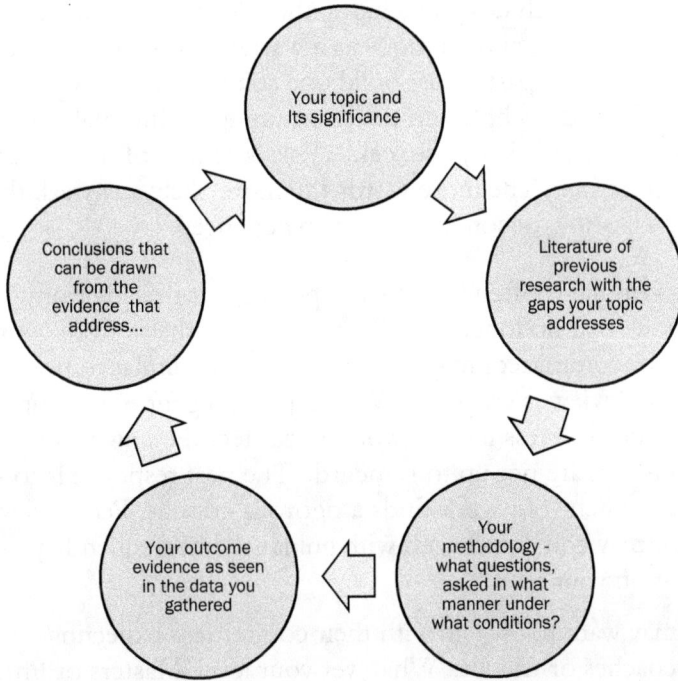

Diagram 1: The flow of research design

This section focuses on thesis building issues and includes an overview of where the process can break down. Some failures may emerge because you misunderstood the process of independent graduate research and stalled out. These can be as deadly as flaws in the actual design of your study.

For example, students may get caught in a pre-proposal loop because they lack clarity about research design or the criteria they are striving to meet. For others, working independently brings up unexpected challenges and it may seem as though proposal review becomes a never ending loop of writing, revision and review without advancing much, even over long periods of time. This is discouraging for both student and committee members. It is the nature of review that the professors examine each iteration as a new document, rather than querying the student process or what underlies the conceptual problems they see. Remember, you can have all the parts and still fail to make your point, in other words, your argument.

The basics. Research design includes: the background, the significance, literature as evidence, and methods as a warrant for success. The design must convince. The parts must build one solid whole. Any deviation of any section from the whole and the structure fails. Internal consistency can seem subtle but is key to success. This is as true of a research paper as of a dissertation. The more words the more likely any weak thread in your logic will show to someone more experienced.

Academic critique is often finding and pulling out threads from conversations that no longer fit. Review of your thesis from your professors or committees may be given a critique similar to peer review for journals. Review is crisp and the critique stringent. Your supervisor is paid to find weakness in your work, to protect the university from publications that are not up to standard. The best response is to say "thank you" when your work finds a rigorous critique. Peer review is not guidance, it may come packaged with guidance but frequently you have to find that on your own.

Students may want to engage with their committees expecting teachers/coaches or friends. Whatever your level, Masters or PhD, be prepared to negotiate for your needs, to want additional support past what is offered and to engage in outside professional development.

Exercise. A simple exercise to get you started and comfortable with the research design process is to map out the parts in the bubbles in Diagram 1 above.

The minimum research design argument. Looking at research design through the lens of building an argument is helpful. The overall message of the proposal is threefold. First, the claim that your research ideas are significant enough to be worthy of the work involved in doing the research. Second, the evidence that the research ideas are based upon literature in the field and where there is a gap, disagreement, or other reason that this new research will add to the entire field of study. Third, the warrant that the methodology is the foundation for the study will provide evidence to fill the gaps delineated. Of course, this must be written up in a manner to convince the committee that you are savvy or skilled enough to achieve the results.

If these goals are attained, the conclusion should be that the proposal may proceed. You might find that designing each chapter as an argument, with claim evidence and warrants, will do much to strengthen the flow. The background claims the study is significant, the literature claims the study builds on the past and is needed in the future, the methodology claims the study will deliver results.

Exercise for anyone having trouble getting the proposal approved. If your work is tied up at the proposal stage, it is probable that something in one or more of these argument parts is missing or that there are inconsistencies between them. Perhaps the literature does not back up the methodology, or the significance is not believable. Your ideas might be fine but the written document awkward, therefore not backing up your claim that you are ready to move to the next phase.

In order to ensure that you, your proposed research methodology, and your writing all meet a credible standard:

1. First, analyze just your title and the headings in your table of contents – Do you see the argument that needs to be in each section? How can these be strengthened?
2. Second, read just the transitions between sections and headings (e.g., introductory and summary paragraphs). Consider adding a sentence or two, one of summation and one that leads your reader onward, to better guide the argument(s) you are making.
3. Practice defending your main and chapter arguments by discussing them with others. Is there a place where, even to yourself, they sound weak? Tighten those areas up.

Additional resources.

- **Finding your topic, what to consider:** https://pd.education/research-design-video-snippets/video/191-finding-your-phd-dissertation-or-thesis-research-topic-what-to-consider.html
- **Video about research questions:** https://pd.education/research-design-video-snippets/video/218-questions-about-research-questions.html

Defending Your Ideas

Whether in class or during your defense or viva you will need to present and discuss your ideas with others. It may be helpful to consider how people who work in universities treat ideas and each other.

The academic environment. Fields of study are based on ideas which mature over time and the test of strength of those ideas is whether they stand up to critique by others. There is nothing personal in this and there is no room for emotion when someone else is trying to dismiss what you just said as fallacious in some manner. Separate yourself from your ideas and allow them to stand on their own, then be prepared to listen to others' comments and come back with alternatives. These conversations help you build your arguments, a helpful skill across most work environments.

However, if a pattern develops and single individuals consistently attack your work in a manner where you leave the exchange feeling diminished then action may be required. Bullies come in many forms and if these people have power over your work, you should consider telling your graduate Dean about the situation.

Another consideration is the difference between the work environment of the university and industry. In business, output is what counts and, for that, work must proceed efficiently. Therefore, people work together in teams, putting aside or working through difference of opinion in order to build results. Contrast this with an academic environment in which the output that counts is frequently the solitary pursuit of research. Other processes can take a long time, ideas can be the only tangible result and are therefore nebulous, and people have developed the patience to allow for that. The maturation of ideas propels the changes in the field frequently taking decades to come about. Industry vs academia represent two different worldviews and expectations.

Students tend to have expectations closer to those of industry. You are there for the output and, if you are a doctoral candidate, the output is the dissertation and graduation. Therefore, you may hope for your committee to be supportive at least as much as critical, guiding as much as critiquing, taking time to explain rather than merely review. The supervisor or advisor works in an academic environment, where time drifts, may respond slowly, causing you difficulties. If you find this the case, see the next chapter and the discussion on negotiation.

Presenting your ideas. You might want to practice the following:

1. Quickly present your ideas to others as an argument.
2. Separate your sense of self from your work. Learn to be objective.
3. Discuss your ideas or work with other colleagues, working with them to objectively root out weakness.
4. Look up common questions asked during defense (or viva if you are in Europe). These illustrate the way researchers pattern their ideas.
5. Rehearse your answers and the situation in which you will need to defend your ideas.
6. Stay objective and calm so you won't become defensive.

In reality, hard questions may be unexpected, especially when they come from committee members who have been supportive up until that time. This will set anyone back. If this happens, take a breath, move back into your objectivity and then answer.

Exercise. A proven way to test the coherence of your research is to finish these seven sentence stems, limiting your response to just that one sentence each.

The sentence stems are:

1. The background to my study is…
2. My research is significant because…
3. The literature on which it is based …
4. The research design employed was…

And if you are preparing for final defense…

1. My results were…
2. I concluded that…

Video resources.

- **How to ace the final defense or viva:**
  https://pd.education/file-downloads/academic-hacks-tools/161-how-to-ace-the-viva-2.html

- **Video exercises on surviving your viva or final defense:** https://pd.education/videos/must-watch-videos/video/123-surviving-your-final-defense.html

Bias

All human beings approach the world through a set of biases that developed from our own personal experiences. The challenge in defense is to understand how those affect our science. How and what you think determines what you allow yourself to observe or consider. Your thoughts color the preconceptions you have about reality. Culture, motivation, history, and training all create biases. You can think of it like a train. Your current understanding of the facts of your life is the sum of those parts. The size and weight they hold on your thoughts create your perspective and that puts boundaries around what you will and will not consider. These boundaries hamper your judgement and keep your current ideas active while working against new thoughts entering and changing what you see, think, do and feel. The more you understand your biases, the less likely they will impinge on your work.

The basics. The most common bias is conformational. These are where you only see what you want to see, what agrees with our cultural motivations and desires. Algorithms heighten the potential for conformational bias to color our lives when the internet feeds back results that agree with our previous searches and click throughs. This has created the concern that our worldview is increasingly limited because of technology and conformational bias.

Consciousness breaks through conformational bias. You need to embrace and consider that which contradicts your world view and way of thinking. Conformational bias coexists with observational selection bias (you only study that which agrees with you), and anchoring effect bias (you don't look for that which does not agree with you), both of which interfere with open data collection and analysis and can be deadly to the accuracy of your work.

Other types of bias keep us feeling safe because they agree with what others around us think (in-group bias) or substantiate past decisions without question (Buyers' Stockholm bias). Bias that keeps you feeling part of the majority is the bandwagon effect bias where you follow the ideas of others despite contrary evidence.

Bias limits thinking and awareness and is contrary to long term success. This is why it is both necessary and difficult to work in cross cultural and diverse teams. No one escapes. Learning more about these habits of thought will allow you to have a better chance to move past them.

Exercise. Consider having to build a scientific study in a neighborhood of people very different from you in culture, socioeconomics, and employment. Now muse about your strengths and deficits. Why might they like you and agree to participate in your project? In what ways would they find you strange and off putting? Do you dress and talk like them? Use the same language in the same way? Does a situation where you are either alone or in a large group cause tension or discomfort? These are at the edge of your biases.

Follow that train of thought until you feel uncomfortable. When you uncover ideas you hold about how others perceive you, then you are close to bias. Thoughts based on (perhaps false) assumptions, centered on the perceptions of others, limit your response patterns. To make up for the limitation your brain cooks up a scenario about "how the world is." This introduces bias.

Video resources.

- **Biases in Your Research:** https://pd.education/research-design-video-snippets/video/140-biases-in-your-research.html

Chapter Three

The Cognitive Skills You'll Need

Building on the last chapter, this one considers five cognitive skills you need in graduate school (and beyond). This chapter closes with skills to get you your next job and a proven strategy to manage big projects while carrying on a busy life, both of which are necessary to help you advance. Most sections conclude with links to video resources.

Note: You might consider rating yourself 1-5 on each of these as to your current perceived level of development. Then proceed to work on one at a time (maybe one per semester). Over time, with just minimal attention, you will find you notice these qualities in others and take them on yourself.

Intelligence

How others rank your intelligence may determine your research opportunities or jobs. Academics take pride in intelligence, and how others see you has a lot to do with the skills you apply cognitively, your perceptions and/or approaches to situations. I had a doctoral student tell me he wanted the degree because all his life people had told him he was stupid, and he wanted to prove them wrong. In 2016, World Economic Forum (WEF) defined the skills they see as critical in the current world context of the fourth Industrial Revolution. When taken together, they define the intelligent person of the future. Anyone skilled in these 10 areas will pass the smart test.

Of these ten, the five cognitive skills, discussed below, include: creativity, flexible cognition, complex problem-solving, and critical thinking, as well as judgment/decision-making. They are all useful in both academic environments and throughout the rest of life. They are outlined here bridging both academia and industry. The five attitudinal skills that complete the WEF list are covered in the next chapter.

Creativity

Creativity, which includes the ability to transfer and transpose ideas into a new context in a manner that appears original, is a core skill in business and academia. Creativity is needed in systems approaches to research, business, culture, the sciences, etc. Creative output will set you apart in graduate school and win the mentor support you need. Impress people with sound, creative solutions or novel approaches based on an innovative conceptual framework. It is fun to be creative, requiring the best of us.

Why is creativity so far reaching and important? It allows you to build bridges in your mind that cut across mental constructs and root out new options for innovation, and thereby increases your sense of self-worth. You don't have to build big projects, paint pictures, or write books to consider yourself creative. Every time you try out a new system or solve a problem in a new way, looking for improvement you engage your creativity muscle. It is a general intellectual ability and one which you all should develop simultaneous to the rest of your graduate skills.

The basics. Creativity requires that you have tolerance for uncontrolled results. When trying something new you are never certain what the outcome will be. Uncertainty requires cognitive fortitude to take risk without attachment to outcome. Once you develop that flexibility, then each new trial becomes an experiment where you build on past results. Positive outcomes help build future levels of self-trust and allow for more risk.

Creativity is also a habit of mind that involves taking a wider focus and incorporating parts and pieces of processes from disparate contexts. Those people that follow the Gardner (2006) theoretical base of intelligences would suggest that to heighten your creativity you cross-pollinate your endeavors in or with other intelligences which are not your natural forte. The realms of intelligence range from musical intelligence to the intelligence involved in self-understanding. The creativity gained from thinking across constructs is a mainstay for the next skill: flexible cognition.

Exercise. Creativity is a process of thought. To replicate results or communicate the process to others it is useful to track your sources. You might test your creative process by:

1. Analyzing a situation that needs a new solution. Write down how you would describe it and what you think is needed in a new solution.
2. Widening your field of thought past the context of the problem. Where else are there situations that result in similar problems? How are they or might they be resolved? Spin out a list of possible and wild ideas.
3. Plotting the potential incorporation of those ideas into the existing situation.
4. Looking for potential points where the new solution(s) might fail.
5. Discussing your ideas with a diverse group of other people. Involving or incorporating the widest set of solutions.
6. Testing those most likely to be adopted and recording results.
7. Replicating or testing other potential solutions as appropriate.

Video resources.

- https://pd.education/job-prep-video-snippets/video/104-creativity.html

Flexible Cognition

No one learns when their minds are made up. Flexible cognition is a key skill when we are learning new things. Employers don't advance someone who only produces common ideas and processes. You are in graduate school to take on new thoughts and incorporate new ideas in your skills. Let those specific lessons branch out into having a flexible approach to thinking about any task you take on. Someone who considers several options rather than going with the first one orwho knows how to risk their comfort so they can embrace a new approach will be the innovator that others are looking for, someone who will advance their field. Flexible cognition is important. The pace of change in every industry requires it.

"Successful behavior requires actively acquiring and representing information about the environment and people and manipulating and using those acquired representations flexibly to optimally act in and on the world" (*Rubin et al., 2014, page 1*). Perhaps you have a topic you acknowledge as out of reach because you did not learn it early enough? Something you do not do, that you have never tried? Think of the person who does not travel because they have no facility with language, or the employee who is never offered advancement. These failures are frequently linked to a lack of flexibility.

Keeping nimble of mind has many benefits. Strong cognitive flexibility allows you to face unexpected situations with calm and centeredness. During crisis or change it increases your likelihood of success because you consider new options rather than repeating old patterns. Flexibility keeps you on the productive side of any spectrum. In an academic world, it's the basis of problem-solving because without it work becomes stale. Over the course of a lifetime the more flexible you are the less stress impacts health and wellbeing (*Gabrys, et al., 2018*).

The basics. Flexible cognition requires growth in attitudes, memory, and a mental capacity to change your perspective. Once we move past our initial inhibitions, each new topic we consider requires us to embrace new patterns of thought inherent in those solutions. For instance, every language comes packaged with its culture's preconceptions about what is important and how people relate. Every field of study also has patterns of thought; a STEM scientist will approach a common topic differently than a social scientist.

Once we have embraced new underlying thoughts and perspectives, we need the mental capacity to switch off from one realm, context or type of thought to another. The next step is to be able to hold them all together, to consider the pros and cons of each. This may require we develop nonlinear patterns of thought and maintain a high level of working memory, as well as a wider worldview. People use tools to aid them in these considerations

Exercise. Inherent in building cognitive flexibility is a comfort with tension or taking on new behaviors. Not only is it a good practice to try new things, it is helpful to repeat them until you are proficient. Change is not only uncomfortable but also invigorating. The ability to take it on and grow develops over time.

For this exercise, take three things from the following list and test them until you feel you have mastered their intricacies.

- Alter your daily routine to incorporate a new behavior or habit.

- Say yes to something you would have previously said no to. Keep doing it until comfortable.
- Do a few tasks each day with your weaker hand until you notice increased muscle control.
- Transfer learning or processes from one situation to another and test the results.
- Meditate for the first time if you don't already practice or try a new style if you do. Continue until you feel the benefits.
- Do strenuous aerobic activity for three minutes three times during the day and repeat each day until you are no longer winded.
- Listen to your inner self talk and reverse what you are telling yourself. Work out of the new perspective and continue trial and error until you see positive change.
- Build an inner picture of success out of something you are worried about, then proceed. Reflect on your results and do it again in another circumstance.
- Listen to a new music that you think you hate, until you have identified 3-5 positive aspects of which you were not aware.
- Go see a movie that or watch a TV show in which you have no interest and look for parts you enjoy. Continue doing this twice a month until you can speak about new genres in entertainment.

Video resources.

- https://pd.education/job-prep-video-snippets/video/22-cognitive-flexibility-and-creativity-a-path-to-success.html
- https://pd.education/job-prep-video-snippets/video/248-cognitive-flexibility.html

Complex Problem Solving

Academic writing, critical thinking, critical analysis, research design, etc. all require the ability to engage in solving problems. But what if the problems are ill-defined or could be addressed through multiple and competing perspectives? This is the definition of complex problems, those which may have multiple partial solutions requiring iterative execution cycles. Even tougher than complex problems, wicked problems require solutions that, by definition, cannot be arrived at using linear thought, are not rational, and compound the difficulties in complexity with irrationality (*Rittel & Weber, 1973*). Both are inherent in a world in which every industry is changing due to technology. Such problems require a tolerance for ambiguity, uncertainty, and the ability to move ahead while living a complex life. These types of problems cannot be solved by one person, working alone. Complex problem solving requires new disciplines of both thought and action.

The basics. In complex situations we must question and remain skeptical to detect and attend to the issues that require further investigation, as well as information that flies in the face of our personal biases. Therefore, working in diverse groups is so important, especially when you want to innovate. Even though often uncomfortable due to diverse styles and manners, the more diversity in a group working on a complex situation, the more likely they will be successful moving forward with a solution (*Hong & Page, 2004*).

A complex problem defies definition. Multiple interactions are embedded in the context, no outcome is clear, and it is unlikely changing only one context will bring resolution. Because of the interrelationship between all of the moving parts even when we are clear about our goal, the interaction between that goal and the parts, makes the situation fuzzy and difficult.

Humans are not good at maintaining strength during times of long-term uncertainty. This exacerbates the likelihood of failure when addressing complexity. Don't try to reduce issues to simple solutions just to alleviate tension? Dorner's (1996) landmark work confirmed that decision-making under these conditions creates failure. His suggestion is to make small decisions, take short term actions, and then carefully watch for the unintended consequences.

Exercise. The following steps should help you identify and work through a complex situation. To start, think of an issue in your field that is either highly contested or considered to be unsolvable.

1. Explore and understand the situation. This requires information retrieval and integration and should be a group process.

2. Work out a representation or formula describing the problem which the people in the group are agree to as a summation. This discussion allows for the surfacing of all the moving parts from the positions of the people in the group. The skills required are the ability to model the problem, develop a hypothesis, and imagine a goal satisfactory to the group.
3. Plan and execute a small action towards that goal. This requires your ability to plan, decide, and act. Dorner, (1996) proved that failure is a plan executed and forgotten.
4. Monitor and reflect continuously as you go forward. The single most important aspect of working with complex or wicked problems is that you continue to take small actions rather than big ones and you monitor, reflect, and adjust as you proceed.
5. Start again whenever the situation changes or new information surfaces. Readjusting action must be parallel with new understanding.

Additional resources.

1. **Wickedness discussed:**
   https://aese.psu.edu/research/centers/cecd/engagement-toolbox/problems/complex-or-wicked-issues
2. **Complex problem-solving step by step, a video:**
   https://pd.education/job-prep-video-snippets/video/152-complex-problem-solving-step-by-step.html

Critical Thinking.

The single skill set that will differentiate you as a Masters or Doctoral graduate from non-graduate applicants for jobs is your ability to think critically about what you read, the problems you solve, etc. The more education you have, the more you should be able to dig into the nuances in a situation, unpack complexity and subtlety, and consider it from all angles. Merged with solid skills in investigating literature, this elevates the likelihood of achieving a workable design or outcome and can be invaluable to employers. Make the most of it in your next job hunt!

We all know people who are good, even great, at one thing. We would go to them for that skill or thought pattern. However, unless they see the big picture, they are limited in their usefulness. Critical thinking involves both the ability to investigate and understand the big picture, and an appreciation for when single-minded focus is the skill necessary to get the job done. It is likely that as you think more critically, your solutions also compel you to learn more widely, in order to personally implement the actions needed.

Critical thinking is a habit of mind. As mentioned in the last section, tension drives us to adopt solutions, even if they are not well considered. A critical mind investigates, considers and reflects, then employs action. Strive to combine critical thought with considered action and to be able to do both well.

The basics. To analyze is the ability to take something apart, look at the pieces, interpret and then explain what you see. Because, as individuals we all come to a problem with a different context, our critical analysis will be unique from others. Working in groups makes it easier. As everyone explains to others how they see the situation the group can infer, and reach wider conclusions based upon group evidence and reasoning.

Exercise. The essence of critical thinking is looking at a situation from many angles. Take for instance some area of your life where you have a problem. Then ask the following questions

- What's happening here?
- Why is this important?
- Who is this important to? Are they involved now?
- What is not obvious or hidden?
- What data exist?
- Can I form a written explanation? Would others agree to it?
- How do I know those things, what is the evidence?
- What have I missed?
- What if…?

Video resource.

- **Critical thinking video snippets:**
  https://pd.education/criticality-video-snippets/video/147-critical-thinking.html

Judgment and Decision-Making

Humans make judgements all the time. Often, they are based on bias and misconception or lead to simplistic actions that fail. Part of graduate school is to help you build cognitive strength in the area of judgement and decision making. Decisions are more instant, while a judgment determines an entire trajectory of action. Good judgment requires oversight and the ability to imagine ahead to determine which roads are likely to take you where you want to go, and which will lead to dead ends. Judgement is a building block of leadership. A judgement is an opinion on which you are ready to decide a course of action. Your decision may be first to investigate that situation to revisit options and then judge what action is needed

The basics. Judgment is a skill, a process, and a product. As is skill, judgment is the ability to effectively decide and come to a sensible conclusion about next actions. Your critical ability to distinguish relationships between things is key. As a process, judgement is something we do both reflectively and as part of a collaborative group. Critically applying your cognitive understanding and seeing something from multiple angles and then drawing sound conclusions after deliberation, comparison, and assessment builds this skill. Judgment can also be a product as in, "that person has good judgment." That implies that over time the opinions, conclusions and determinations of that person consistently produce positive results.

When judging and making decisions there are assumptions we can make. One is that there is an uncertainty of outcome. There also may be uncertainty in whether you have all the information that you need. As with previous cognitive skills, the first strategy should be to look at the situation from all angles and to collaborate with a group of people that have experience and can help. This leads to the second assumption which is that the decision-maker must have the ability to take in the whole picture, get past their own personal preferences and draw the conclusions needed to move forward. When in a highly complex situation either or both of those two assumptions may not be true.

Judgment assesses risk. Risk assessment includes objective and subjective analysis of the probabilities of outcome of the certain actions

41

we take. Just as in ethical review, good judgment incorporates the risks and benefits to all parties, in addition to the probability of reaching the immediate goal.

There are several things that cause errors in judgment. For example, not being as aware, as ethical, or rational. Self interest leads to confirmation bias. A problem might be framed incorrectly. Overconfidence also causes error.

Exercise. If you want to test your judgement and decision-making, consider a situation around which you need to make a decision, preferably one that has multiple options. Test yourself by following all the steps below and see if you come to more possible decisions than were originally apparent.

1. Mind map the situation, identifying the complexity and interrelationship of the parts and stakeholders. Include at least one other person in this brainstorming.
2. Talk it over with another person.
3. Search out information that disagrees with your first analysis or adds a conflicting possibility. Use that to identify other alternative pathways.
4. Consider among yourselves what you are seeing, weigh the evidence.
5. List alternative courses of action.
6. Do a risk and benefits assessment for each alternative.
7. Make a judgment about which has the most benefit for the least risk.
8. Take small actions and evaluate their outcomes.
9. Re-review and revisit your decisions as you understand the unintended consequences.

Video resource.

- **Judgment and decision-making video:**
  https://pd.education/job-prep-video-snippets/video/151-judgement-and-decision-making.html

Chapter Four

Three Key Ideas on Writing (and the Importance of Data)

You will spend much of your time in graduate school writing. As you reflect on the first two sections of this chapter, your ideas about writing and your work will become more sophisticated. When you build on that sophistication and incorporate the importance of data and you will have incorporated much of the full graduate mindset.

Voice

You are not the person sitting next to you. Even when assigned the same specific task, your work will be unique. As you move beyond graduate school into whatever work and life awaits you, it is important to reflect on that uniqueness. In a global environment filled with lots of voices, this becomes even more critical in order to stand out in a global marketplace.

Considerations needed to develop your voice fall into three areas. These are your passions, your style (which includes what you emphasize and your values) and the structure(s) you impose on your thinking and writing.

Passion in writing. People who think of academic writing as dry, may have difficulty in considering passion in research. But how can this be true? Think of the following: a Nobel Peace Prize scientific prizewinner, a scientist doing a Ted talk or a graduate student giving a three-minute thesis. All are examples of someone doing scientific work, who are dedicated to their work. Passion, therefore, must be an integral part of any final writing in graduate school, or you will have missed the mark.

Writing with Passion

What is passion? It is focused caring. And what is it that scientists and academic writers need to care about? Six things come to the fore…

We need to care about our subject. While as scientists we are constrained to research and take into account not only our opinions but those that differ from us, this does not mean that we don't have opinions, or driving force behind why we are doing what we are doing. At the most basic level scientists believe that their research will develop into answers to questions, or advances forward in their fields, which are important. Those answers drive passion.

Writers must care about whether readers can comprehend their ideas. This requires you spend a little time thinking about your readership, or, if you have several types of readers, you understand the differences in the writing necessary to reach them. There are many examples of scientists who write for their field in the most academic language and simultaneously bridge the gap to the general population. They tend to write twice, once in journals and then by taking that same scientific work and explaining it in more common terms. Another example of this are the Masters and PhD students who are completing scientific research in one type of academic language, while presenting their work in a three-minute thesis competition. If you have the opportunity on your campus to attend, you'll see science designed to reach a non-scientific audience.

You not only want your readers to understand your ideas, you want them to use them. In research this is building a convincing argument with recommendations, in the marketing world this is a "call-for-action." Academic voice encompasses an awareness of where you hope your reader will go or how they might use your work. You build this throughout by what you emphasize, plotting the breadcrumbs you want your audience to follow. In a final research thesis or dissertation, key thoughts or "golden threads" that ensure the trail from beginning to end is clear. Complex work requires several threads, or main points, woven together to build a tapestry of ideas and methods which results in a clear and readable scientific document. The way in which you weave these threads together, is a main aspect of your voice.

Passion also involves caring about the long-range focus and outcomes in your field of study. As an example, social science should benefit mankind by advancing its understanding of itself. STEM practitioners are involved in concrete, usually physical measurements and solutions. Sometimes personal voice can impact an entire field, Martin Seligman is an example of this in psychology. When he was president of the American Psychological Association, in (1998) he helped empower a shift of focus from deficit research to studying what is constructive. Positive psychology took its place in a field that had previously focused attention on negative psychological attributes or problems.

Since we care about our field we also need to uphold or challenge the standards of that field. This requires not only skill and use of language but also philosophical and theoretical insight. Linguists don't write like biologists or engineers. Social scientists focus on different populations and have different values about humanity than do psychologists or anthropologists. All fields are constrained by standards. It behooves you, as the future of your field, to analyze those standards and decide if you agree with them based on your values. A goal is for your work to shine as an example of what you believe. Should your passion and voice lead you to challenge the manner in which things are commonly done, those resulting variations establish your voice.

Given that we live in a global environment and that the boundaries between scientific thought and what is understood in the general population are blurring, it behooves all academics to consider what it would take to attract a wider range of readers as an audience to their ideas. Attracting a wide range of audience also means that you are likely to publish in more than one form, some written and others on media. In a knowledge economy where individuals both in and out of academia have little time, video and voice communication have become a more common way to publish ideas and attract others to them. Part of the graduate degree is the invitation to become someone whose voice is strong and whose ideas are worthy of much wider range of discussion.

Style, emphasis and values. Three elements of writing incorporate your caring and passion about your topic into your academic voice: style, emphasis, and values. Style develops as you develop an understanding of the needs and desires of the readership you wish to attract. You may end up with more than one style. As an example, most of my speaking and writing, like the writing that you have experienced in this book, are a casual voice overlaid on academically driven ideas. I use a more rigorous, less personal, academic voice when I write for journals. When

I was a young academic I struggled. My comfort with the casual created doubt because it seemed as though everyone else's writing was more evolved than mine. I understood that the voice which I want to be identified with is the same as a person would expect if they sat down with me and they were asking for personal support. On the other hand, my arguments must be strong to compensate for prejudice of voice from colleagues. I stand for language that conveys complex thoughts with pragmatic clarity, through examples, etc.

You may work within a context in which only use of the specific language of that context will gain them entry. If that is the case, then that must dictate your style. Engineers speak and write differently than biologists as an example. When both write for their fields the documents that evolve are not generally accessible to a wider population.

Within any given scientific document there are many things that can be emphasized. These are often your findings and discussion, but not always. If you have an interesting nuance on the methodology, as another example, you might want to emphasize that. An easy way to know what threads your work might advance is to examine the things you care about then emphasize them through use of headings, discussion, etc. throughout your writing. If you critique the headings in this book you will see that they do two things: speak directly to you and deliver a message as to "why you should care about this section".

What you value defines you and should be apparent in your work. This will drive who you become in your field and should dictate your voice. Do you value rigor? Clarity? Readability? Accessible thought? Within your own field, whose work do you gravitate to and what is their voice? Can you use it as a foundation for your own? Take a moment and consider why their work speaks to you, how they frame their ideas, etc., and you will have insight into the values you may want to highlight or maintain throughout your writing.

Structure of thought. Almost all scientific writing has five parts, background, literature, methodology, results, and findings and discussion. So how then does structure come into this question of voice? I like to remind people that writing research argument is an art form, rather than a prescribed pathway. As with any art form, we learn the standards, build our skills, and then we superimpose our ideas on that to make it our own.

Good writers are good readers. Finding and analyzing models of others academic voice will help you develop your own. Watching how others massage the typical structure so that their work emphasizes what they find important will help you make the same decisions. Of course, not all published work is worth reading. Some may have good ideas but a rubbish writing style that puts the reader to sleep. Save examples of those that do both well, so that when you need the reminder of the quality you strive for, you have them on file.

Structure morphs to fit need. A mixed methodologist might need to discuss results from quantitative evidence separately from the qualitative. Someone whose concept of thought drives their theoretical choice might highlight that and spend less time on methodology. As an author you take your readers on a journey. Sometimes a tour guide leaves the main road in order to emphasize something so we might see the enhanced beauty of the whole when we return to it.

A word of caution for new scientists and writers, write to the prescribed norm and be able to do that well, before you test different structures. Why? Because the prescribed five parts will point out to you, or peer reviewers, weaknesses in your argument and you'll get over them quicker. Once your voice has matured, and/or when you have a strong mentor with whom you can discuss the ins and outs of your ideas, you can choose to structure your work more creatively.

Exercise. As you consider the style, emphasis and structure you want to develop, find a few pieces of writing in your field that provoke different responses. Ensure that one is from an author whose work you would like to emulate. Analyze it first by asking the following questions.

1. What about the work engages you? Their ideas? Their style? The mechanics of how they present their argument? Their topic?
2. Do they use first person? Are you addressed as their reader? Or is the writing formal, conservative or held at a distance from the reader?
3. How do they lay out their arguments? Do they follow an established scientific pattern? Do they use examples?

4. What other stylistic or directional difference of voice can you identify between this author and others?

Now repeat the exercise using the work of another author different than the first. If you can, choose examples where one is formal another conservative. Also choose from a selection of publishers, some non-peer reviewed magazines, compared to journals. Investigate work written for a lay population s well as for other academics in your field. Chart your own course based upon your analysis of what you like or to which you respond.

Video resources.

- **Write your passion #1:** https://pd.education/getting-published-video-snippets/video/16-write-your-passion-1.html
- **Write your passion #2:** https://pd.education/getting-published-video-snippets/video/15-write-your-passion-2.html
- **Write your passion#3:** https://pd.education/getting-published-video-snippets/video/13-write-your-passion-3.html
- **Write your passion #4:** https://pd.education/getting-published-video-snippets/video/14-write-your-passion-4.html

Data, Charting Your Future

This chapter wraps up by discussing the advantages in understanding data as a mainstay of any next employment. When you merge that with the cognitive skills discussed in the last with a well-developed voice and an ability to hone your passion, you have the makings of leadership. I write this with the hope that all my readers find the place in life where their leadership can be let lose to the benefit of their communities and the world.

Appreciation of data. The understanding you develop in graduate school of the necessity for evidence which backs up a claim has multiple implications for your future. First, big data puts a new perspective on the scale of life and the stories told about it as well as uncovering previously unknown ethical issues. Working with data changes a person's perspective and lessons the likelihood of being swayed by fallacious assumptions or hearsay. Your training may change you to a skeptic on current affairs, pointing out when data is flawed or seems nonexistent. It becomes less likely you will be taken in by fake news. Hopefully you also will be someone who strives to use the data in your life to innovate in ethical ways.

Merged with cognitive skills. Graduate education gives you an advantage on the five cognitive development skills from the World Economic Forum: creativity, flexible cognition, complex problem solving, critical thinking and judgement/ decision-making as discussed in the previous chapter. Because of your broader understanding of the literature in your field you can be more creative with how those ideas are used. Because you have become comfortable in an environment of critique your flexible cognition is heightened. Whatever field you are trained in, complex issues abound and now your problem-solving options contain a wider range of potential. Through all your training you were required to maintain a standard of critical thinking which will impact your judgment and decision-making.

Equals leadership? You may also find yourself less likely to take an easy answer, which as discussed before often leads to failure (Dorner, 1996). This is the trait that I hope sets you up to be a leader in your community. If it is your calling to do so, step up when your logic and heart propel action, this training has given you skills that will unfold in their importance throughout the rest of your life, often in unexpected ways. When these skills come together, they are of strategic importance to our communities, our fields, our families, and our world.

Chapter Five

Develop the Skills that Help You Thrive

Thriving

Human beings evolve in nonlinear patterns. Because we experience our body, mind, and sprit as connected, an impact on one naturally leads to changes in the others. Graduate work not only changes your habits of mind and builds your resiliency muscles, it changes perceptions, awareness and worldview. This chapter takes a holistic approach to the skills graduate students need in order to thrive. Thriving, as defined by psychologist Martin Seligman (2011) includes five elements: **P**ositive emotions, **E**ngagement, **R**elationships, **M**eaning, and **A**chievement (PERMA). Each of these have been the focus of several well-known bodies of research and, if they are of interest, I recommend you investigate them further through the resources referenced at the end of this chapter.

Positive emotions. These include more than mere pleasure or enjoyment, but also, and more importantly in the graduate context, include the pleasures that come from being intellectually challenged and having the fortitude to stand up to those challenges. Positive emotions stretch the imagination. Because this is true, focusing on the instances when you are challenged will help you override or undo negative experiences. As you will see, this compliments Carol Dweck's work (*Dweck & Yeager, 2019*) on mindset and Angela Duckworth's (*Duckworth et.al, 2007*) on grit. Both will help you thrive.

Engagement. This is your ability to become absorbed in your work to the point where you lose your sense of time which is also discussed by Mihaly Csikszentmihalyi (2020) in his work on "flow." Flow is total engagement. It is a is natural state when you're engaged in activities that have three qualities: you lose track of time, you feel calm and centered, and the activity is centered in something you do well. You may drop into flow when, you are accomplished enough at the task that you feel comfortable, yet there's a little bit of outside pressure or challenge. This mix creates a situation where your enjoyment is high, and you lose any sense of time.

Relationships. These are meaningful to humanity as we are hard wired as social beings, relying on each other for survival (*Dutton & Ragins, 2007*). Graduate school may offer both fleeting and long-term relationships. Look for those that spread happiness, cheer, and laughter because this is an important function for your sense of thriving.

Meaning. This is defined differently by everyone. For some it is a loving relationship, for others it is doing well in a job or having a career that is valuable. How we define value in the world is also completely personal. What remains constant, however, is your need to engage in acts that are larger than yourself. A life with meaning is an effective barrier against depression, or the other challenges that go with non-thriving experiences. Chapter six looks at the five attitudinal skills suggested by the World Economic Forum and in that model a service orientation is one of those skills which goes hand in hand with meaning.

Achievement. Graduating is a positive outcome to an explicit goal, yet the challenge with graduate school is that it is such a long-term objective with so many difficulties to be faced along the way, that the sense of achievement or accomplishment that go with it diminishes. It is important that you celebrate your minor milestones. Professional development helps, as you focus on small gains as well as large achievements.

These are all elements of **eudaemonic** well-being, which goes beyond happiness into the realm of meaning and purpose. Eudaemonic well-being is a psychological orientation to what others call the mind-body-spirit connection (*Fave, et.al., 2013*)

Your Mind Body Spirit Connection

To thrive is to have a strong life spirit, to know that you are on the right track and the world is good. But how do mind and body come into that? This is an important question for graduate students since you will be engaging in work that challenges your mind and are going through stress which may also challenge your body.

Taking the mind, body, spirit connection seriously is relatively new. Since the 1970s we have seen an increase in general knowledge as medical practitioners began researching and publishing studies that pointed to different long-term health outcomes based on lifestyle. One of the most famous is? the Whitehall study of which pointed to workers in low level jobs having higher stress, less autonomy and more than twice the risk of developing metabolic syndromes that are precursors to heart disease and diabetes (*Marmot, & Brunner, 2005*). In the United States, several people have built large and successful research centers based upon the mind-body connection. People like Dean Ornish Clinical Professor of Medicine at the University of California, San Francisco and President and Director of the Preventive Medicine Research Institute in Sausalito, or Dr Deepak Chopra, Physician and Director of the Chopra Center for Wellbeing, would be examples. Many medical schools and centers now have departments devoted to mind-body research with NIH funding more than a thousand projects at over 200 institutions looking into these connections

A tale of two students. What goes wrong if you don't pay attention to the body, mind connection? The obvious and most researched answer to that question is that you get sick. Two different options exist, depending on your connection to your life spirit. Let's say you have just entered your degree program and taken a class or two. You become excited by all the new things you're learning, and although you find some of it difficult, such as the writing, you apply yourself 120%. This leads to long hours. You get tired. Some of the later work seems more confusing and working harder is no longer giving you the edge you need. You feel depleted. You come across people in class who have many more skills than you do. You become worried or anxious. And the next thing you know you are sick. Perhaps the same situation develops in reverse. You find out you or a family member is sick. You begin to worry about the diagnosis. Suddenly it's hard to focus in class and new material does not make as much sense. You find yourself falling behind and have lost your motivation. In both of these examples, it was your sense of spirit that diminished over time. Suddenly you didn't have as much access to that which upholds you and makes you feel strong and on the right track.

Another student comes to class and similarly faces either work overload or bad diagnosis. This student however came to school with strong routines, which included daily meditation, regular time outs to clear their head, and spending time with nature. Discipline formed a structure for them. When challenges became tough, their life had ease and grace, with family and friend connections built into it. Even with extreme stressors some students will have a better time of handling them. You may know students like this – hopefully, you are one. These people may seem calm in the face of the storm, happy despite everything, always with a positive spin on the world. These things aren't a result of good genes. They are a result of good habits.

You are responsible for whether you thrive. The graduate experience is not a single track of going to school learning, attending class and completing your degree. Graduate school is a holistic challenge. As your mind learns new things and you embrace an entirely new structure of how you look at the world, you will experience stress that affects your body. Depending on the level of stress and how you handle it, you may find graduate work has thrown off the continuum of your life, therefore impacting your ability to thrive.

This chapter is dedicated to ideas and exercises that help you maneuver through those types of stresses. It gives you exercises to help you consider developing the routines and disciplines that aid a thriving graduate experience. The five attitudinal skills from the World Economic Forum conclude the chapter because they will not only help you as you develop them in graduate life but are of critical importance for your next job.

Depending on your religious background, meditation may not be a descriptor that works for you. Think instead of sitting quietly and listening, of reflecting calmly and letting the totality of your mind-body-spirit speak to you and bring up your highest life potential. Meditation is another way to access the feelings you have when you walk in nature, see a rainbow, look up at a starry night and see the Milky Way, etc. All of these allow us to center on the world and how good it is to be alive. Meditation brings those same feelings close when you set a regular habit of listening. It is beyond the scope of this chapter but there will be additional resources that, should you be interested, could help you build a calm spirit.

Metacognition

What is metacognition? More importantly, why should you pay attention to it? The short and easy answer is that metacognition is thinking about thinking with an eye to improving your mental processes, skills and awareness. Being able to build across all three areas of body mind and spirit is a metacognitive idea and is a first step towards awareness. Increased awareness of the whole structure in which you live is a key foundational platform from which to build both your current graduate and future work life. An important outcome in building metacognition is the ability to switch gears and look at life experience from different perspectives. As you saw in chapter 1, this is also a major component of critical thinking.

Switching mental gears while facing challenges is not easy. It helps to have already developed a growth mindset (*Dweck, & Yeager, 2019*). Dweck investigated why some children learn and others don't. The oversimplified answer turned out to be how they looked at the world and their own ability to learn, she called this *mindset*.

Dweck defined two types of mindset: fixed and growth (2015). Your view of how the world works and your place in it is cemented early in life by the messages you received. If you were told that what you saw was "just how it is, can't change those things" then it is easy to see yourself in the same light. If you were told that even though you failed, you could learn, and would do better next time, then you have an edge on the development of a growth mindset. The good news is that growth can be learned. It is your choice whether to it continue to accept your childhood messages or set them aside and learn a new path.

You may be limited by the foundational idea that you have a certain place in the world, level of intelligence, or set of skills that cannot be changed. I think about my time as a high school teacher and the students who had known each other since kindergarten. One boy had been the bad ass in kindergarten and, while he was maturing out of that role, I could see how his classmates were limiting his growth by playing off him with the expectation to stay in his previous role. You may have had a similar experience where you were growing beyond something and others could not see the changes. The result may have been that you were held back. It is hard, but necessary, to take the harder road and strike out on our own and change.

Learning new skills provides many opportunities to hear the small voice in your head that whispers to you. My mind tells me I can't learn languages because the few times I have tried to speak in new language I found it particularly hard. That voice makes it seem safer for me to say I can't do it, rather than put in the real toil and work it would take to learn a foreign language. Language is my personal example, but everyone probably has one. Is there something you have not cared enough to learn so you have not done the work required to learn it and have just come to accept that, "this is just the way it is"?

A growth mindset involves knowing that we are evolutionary beings and that with work and focus there is nothing our brains won't be able to take on. This doesn't make learning easy, or that you won't face difficulties others might not have to face. An attitude that there is always a way to grow past your current limitations, coupled with an understanding of the particulars of your learning style, and this growth mindset will help you overcome what now may seem insurmountable challenges.

Exercise one. A portion of having and continually maintaining a growth mindset has to do with what our inner voice tells us. In the following exercise you will reflect on those mental (and incorrect) barriers.

- List the things you think you can't do.
- Reflect on why you think you can't do them… (Include your previous experiences, what people said etc.).
- Reflect on what you may be afraid of when you consider learning those skills… (Some possibilities may include not having enough time or money, other people's reactions, etc.).
- Reflect on why you should or want this accomplishment… (Possibilities include positive outcomes in terms of feelings, more structure, money, job opportunities, etc.).
- Define steps you can take right now… (Make it easy, just list a few things that can move your mind onto new possibilities).
- Build a plan for growth… (Including two or three steps are all you need to get started and build momentum. You just have to follow through).

Exercise two. The other side of metacognition is knowing what you are good at and how to employ these skills for your own benefit in uncomfortable settings. The following self-awareness worksheet can get you started and there are other resources listed in the additional resources section

- Off the top your head, what are your three greatest strengths? (Note that in the additional resources section there is a URL that leads you to the University of Pennsylvania site for a number of surveys you can take to test yourself on your strengths and other attributes?). In terms of your graduate work, it is most beneficial, since that is the focus of this worksheet.
- List two or three things that seem easier for you than others in your graduate cohort or class.
- List two or three favorite things you like to do.
- List two or three things that have been big or small recent successes.
- Reflect on what actions you took to make those successes happen?

Now consider taking those skills and changing recent and future outcomes…

- List two or three things that did not go as well as you had hoped.
- Reflect on what you could have done differently to change less than desirable results.
- Reflect on where you could have gone for support?
- Consider new options for support and list them.
- Reflect on whether you are open to sharing your challenges so that others can help? Why or Why not?
- What new opportunities might you consider for ongoing support during your graduate work?
- List two or three things you are not fond of doing yet you think challenges might go more easily if you had these as part of your routines or disciplines.

Additional Resources.

- Go to https://www.authentichappiness.sas.upenn.edu/testcenter for the strengths test and others to see where you rank on variables that equate to thriving.

Routines

Just as keeping a growth mindset is a foundational basis for a strong graduate experience mentally, routine is a strong foundational base for your body. Not enough can be said about the importance of regular sleep, good food, and regular exercise as disciplines on which you can maintain health when life requires you tire yourself out mentally. During the time I was getting my PhD, I would get up and go to the YMCA and do a morning workout. Even though it was difficult to make myself get there, afterwards I always felt stronger and more able to handle the day. The steps to ensuring I got out the door included having my gym bag ready from the night before, eliminating the excuse of not finding my gear or making myself late.

When tired, it is hard to make decisions and easy to collapse in on yourself at home with technology. Positive physical routines can support your system of self-nurturing and social interactions without costing much energy to make them happen. As an example, you may see the same people at the gym. You can feel invigorated by getting off campus and interacting regularly with the rest of the world.

The basics. Routine is more than doing the same thing every day at the same time, although that is part of it. It is also consciously deciding what you need to take care of yourself and plotting a course or way of being that helps your overall health. I'm often struck by the fact that people treat their animals, their children, and their best friends, better than themselves. Imagine the next time you look in the mirror that you are looking at the most important person in your life. Is that person taking care of themselves? Are they getting up early enough to give themselves some time before they start a busy day? Are they meditating? Are they giving themselves space to just be themselves or are they always on the go? How might you suggest they (you) take better care?

The exercise below was designed to help people stop procrastinating and keep focused on work. However, the Pomodoro technique can also be used to help you build a routine of taking care of yourself by enlarging and focusing on the break times for positive health providing habits and activities.

Pomodoro technique. The originators of the Pomodoro technique originally designed 20 minutes on focused activity, five minutes off. Every three or four sessions of on and off were celebrated by a longer time off. For most graduate students, 20 minutes is not adequate to get much done. Probably you also have a longer ability to focus. I use a 50 minute on and 10 minutes off cycle, ensuring that I get up and move once and hour, stretching, etc.

This technique can also be used to build in time for yourself. You'll have to play with the timing, but you might start with 45 minutes on task with 15 minutes off, using the off times as important as the on times for building a routine of self-care. In other words 45 minutes you work on your class work or thesis writing and research, 15 minutes you meditate, get a glass of water, walk around the block, stretch, clear your mind and body before you take on the next section of work.

When my world is particularly busy, I use whiteboards as parking lots, noting thoughts of what needs to be done but not focusing on them. On one are the tasks that have to be done for the work, and on the other is a list of ideas, personal tasks, or new routines, all of which keep me grounded in the life that is my personal life as well as the life that is my mental life. Separating out these differences helps to ensure I do not lose one for the other.

Graduate routines. Consider the following three types of routine behaviors and employ them as you find necessary during your graduate work.

Time management strategies. Top corporate performers think six weeks ahead, using a calendar to map out what needs doing and what outcomes will determine success. You should never let any other competing obligation get in the way of achieving those goals. Whenever you are concerned whether you will meet your deadlines, backwards map from the end to your current time, including the life issues that compete. Too much? It is easier to adjust six weeks ahead of time than at the last minute. Negotiate with family and friends to relieve some of the burden when necessary. More about these ideas in additional resources. A free tool I like to keep all the complexities going the right direction is available from KanBanFlow.com. The paid version gives you the ability for swim lanes, which allow you to plan ahead six weeks.

Network Cultivation. Networks are built over time, weaving in and out of the phases of your life. The bigger and richer they are the more they pay off in unexpected ways. The people you choose to network with may not be people you like or want to hang out with, but there are things you can mutually do for each other. Consider networking a quid pro quo habit and allow your generosity of spirit to show. Be sure to include a librarian in your network, by being a warm and welcoming client you may enrich their day and it is guaranteed that they know tools and hints that will come in handy for your graduate work.

Digital routines. You should build good digital habits from day one. These include ways you collect data on what you read, how you save your files so you can find them later, and how you decide on software, use the cloud and collaborate with others.

Bibliographic software. Choose your bibliographic software carefully and start to use it as soon as you enter graduate school. You want to be able to import accurately, shift outputs according to the academic style required, and easily make notes on everything you read that may be worthy of consideration later. Files should be able to upload to the records and you should be able to make notes there so reading, notes and bibliographic output are held in one place. Finally, you need to be able to group and regroup as you use your references in writing for different types of publication.

Date stamps and backups. Saving a file in progress at least once a week with a different date stamp give you the dual benefit of helping you find a document and giving you a recent backup if something goes wrong on your system. It is often important when revising to be able to go back to investigate earlier versions. While MS Word has some functions that allow for this, date stamping at the beginning of a file name is more dependable. A date stamp such as a file name of 20190726 for July 26th 2019 allows for your memory when looking for an older document to have two search parameters – the title if you remember it and the general year and month you did the work. Backing up to a cloud-based provider automatically such as OneDrive, Dropbox, etc. adds an extra layer of security.

The cost(s) of tools. Your graduate school may provide software for you. In other situations, they may recommend solutions and require you purchase them. As a student you will have options for student discounts, yet graduate life is expensive and students, in our experience, are interested in the most innovative solutions as well as the cheapest. Before you decide to go for new, innovative and / or free or open source tools, or decide to pay for more conservative solutions, consider what your time is worth. Looking into the variety of options takes time. Every type of software takes a while to master. Will the new innovations save you time or make your workflow more easily? What solutions have been around long enough you know they will stay? You do not want to invest everything in a type of solution only to have that company bought out and your documents not portable. Do you need the innovation, or would you do better with a proven workhorse that everyone knows how to use? What software is used by your committee members? This will be important if you will be asking them for feedback on data. A good digital routine is to use the latest versions of the best-known leaders in every technological niche – especially when these are widely known on campus.

On the cloud. Cloud based solutions such as Microsoft 365 will give you updated versions through the year and many of their newest are useful to the research community. Keeping your documents on the cloud as well as your desktop, gives an added level of security. Being conscious of your cloud-based permissions, especially when sharing, lowers the likelihood of your work being plagiarized.

Security and privacy. Because of the added security and privacy issues that come with cloud-based work having a password vault and regularly updating unique passwords is the most secure way forward.

Video resources.

- **Bibliographic software for graduate students:** https://pd.education/academic-writing-video-snippets/video/182-bibliographic-software-for-graduate-students-why-use-it.html

- **PHD use of bibliographic or reference software:** https://pd.education/academic-writing-video-snippets/video/185-setting-up-your-bibliographic-software.html
- **MS Word snippet 1- navigation pane and headings:** https://pd.education/tools-hacks-video-snippets/video/31-ms-word-snippet-1-navigation-pane-and-headings.html
- **MS Word snippet 2 – headings for academic users:** https://pd.education/tools-hacks-video-snippets/video/32-ms-word-snippet-2-headings-for-academic-users.html
- **MS Word snippet 3 – setting up personal tools for academic:** https://pd.education/tools-hacks-video-snippets/video/33-ms-word-snippet-3-setting-up-personal-tools-for-academics.html
- **MS Word snippet 4 – Setting up for a dissertation:** https://pd.education/tools-hacks-video-snippets/video/34-ms-word-snippet-4-setting-up-for-a-dissertation.html
- **MS Word snippet 7 – table of contents for academics:** https://pd.education/tools-hacks-video-snippets/video/37-ms-word-snippet-7-table-of-contents-for-academics.html

Discipline

People fail graduate school because they do not have enough power of spirit behind their decision to pay attention to or persevere past so that they can overcome their shortcomings. This may sound harsh, but I have seen people face horrific difficulty and come through to graduation while others disengage. Some frame these choices as will power but I see it more as power of your life spirit to say no to temptation so you can complete what is necessary to get to your goal. Take for example this, conversation overheard in a coffee shop near campus: First person, "it's summer-time and I just want to relax." Second person, "but I thought you were going to go to the library to get more of your literature review done?"

Whether two people, or two voices in your own head, that conversation will not be unusual for anyone in graduate school. On the one hand, you need to have some time off in relaxation or you will find yourself overly anxious and in difficulty, due to fatigue and maybe anxiety. On the other hand, without discipline, that voice can overshadow and eventually overtake your success. If your discipline includes disciplined routines to take good care of yourself, then you can have them both.

What about procrastination? We all have an inner voice that leads us to do things which are completely nonproductive. Why did I think that dessert would make me feel better? What is the joy in social media? Why did I watch every Netflix trailer? You probably have other ways you procrastinate. Whatever it is: social media or zoning out watching television, people procrastinate for several underlying reasons. You may be facing a difficult challenge that you want to avoid. Perhaps the trajectory towards the goal is over a long time (like years) without clear deadlines? Then it is easy to give in to that voice. Perhaps, the steps to get you there are unclear? In all these cases, discipline will help you stay the course.

I personally define discipline as when my true self, the portion of me that is strong, compassionate and knows what my next step should be, has a voice, guides my actions, and helps me move toward the best outcome. Whether it is the discipline to say "no" to distractions that have little benefit or the discipline to say, "Yes, I must do this now," and take action, hearing that voice and listening is important. Discipline is what gets you up a half an hour to an hour earlier than the rest of your family so you can get your graduate work done in peace and quiet. Discipline is what moves you to start on your projects, classwork etc. early, rather than waiting till the last minute when you must rush. Discipline is the wise sensible voice that gives you the grit to finish any project that is multi years in length. Your graduate work is not just two years or five years, it is a day after day exercise of discipline. Are you ready for it? If not, the following exercise may help

Exercise. Get out a piece of paper or open a journal and make three columns.

- In the first column on the left-hand side of the sheet write down the words you associate with discipline.
- Put a mark by all the words that have a negative connotation for you.

- After the words you have marked, write their opposite in the second column. For instance, if you had written 'regulation' as a synonym for discipline and that word has a negative feeling for you then you might put freedom or readjustment.
- Now consider the positive side of that continuum. In the third column, reflect on the role in establishing new routines and making them a discipline where, because of your new strength, you experience more freedom. For instance, to have discipline is to embrace strength and forethought in order to build a strong life.
- Write down three ways you might be more disciplined and the strength that you might expect from these habits.
- Choose one and implement it for a week. If it feels good, take on another.

Building New Habits

Our habits determine how others see us. I'm not talking about the small habits of whether you take milk in your coffee, but the habits of personality such as whether you habitually tell the truth no matter what the consequences. They underlie everything and they make growth easy or hard depending on whether they support strength or not. Habits impact metacognition, routine, and discipline. When you investigate how your habits affect body, mind, and spirit you see they are indicators of future success or failure. To use a graduate school example, some students habitually persist no matter what challenges they face, while others habitually give up and stop before they reach their goals. Habits set circumstances and skills in motion that result in consistent types of outcomes.

You have habits of body, mind and spirit. They have been created by regular patterns within the context of your life and have become hardwired through repetition. Building the habits and disciplines ahead of when you really need their support, is the ideal but is not always possible. Habits take time, can be easily broken, and, ultimately, determine who we are. A wise person once told me, "it's not how well you do it, it is how will you get back to doing it? When you've stopped." In my life, this habit of starting again, let's call it dogged determination, whether about something mundane like eating well or making more profound changes such as upgrading my ability to listen empathetically, or finishing this book, has made all the difference.

Habits also define much of your potential as they either support or get in the way of your goals. Since graduate school is an opportunity for growth, working to become more than you are now, the following can help you avoid traps of your own making. Social networks help build success in graduate school and collegial habits are important as well. To help you investigate your habits, look over this list which contains both character traits that help you meet challenges and those that aid who you choose as colleagues and friends.

Exercise. Consider the following continuums of positive versus negative habits. Give yourself a one for being clearly on the left, a two for somewhere in the middle and a three for being on the right.

- Persistent? Or Inconsistent?
- Having grit? Or Holding back?
- Disciplined? Or Impulsive?
- Empathetic listener? Or Self-absorbed?
- Accurate and precise? Or Vague and casual?
- Writing and speaking with clarity and precision? Or Casual and non-impressive?
- Open to others? Or Closed off and isolated?
- Curious and analytic? Or Dull and unconcerned?
- Active questioning? Or Passive acceptance?
- Posing problems and bringing solutions? Or "Letting it slide"
- Broad thinker? Or Single minded?
- Ability to transfer? Or Lack of creativity?
- Reflective and reasoned? Or Non reflective and unthoughtful?
- Responding with awe and wonder? Or Existing within a dull routine?
- Risk-taking? Or Avoiding change?
- Sharing humour and caring? Or Harsh or uncaring?

How many 1's have you marked on the left How does that compare to the number of 3's on the right? Is this how you want to be seen by others? Consider your appearance to others and whether you are exhibiting the characteristics you want to be known for. Since few know each other well, in the graduate environment you have the option of testing out new ways of being. Consider people who you might want to emulate, reflect on how they exhibit the traits you admire, and then put into action the positive changes you desire.

Looking at your earlier list, mark the numbers around which you wish to grow. The following six exercises should kick off building new habits of body-mind-spirit. Choose one or two from the list above that you feel will make the biggest difference in achieving your goals. Then drill down to something specific you want to change. Most habits begin small and build with time to become routines or disciplines. If you find that you backslide, don't give yourself a hard time, just start again. Eventually you'll find there is a longer and longer time between restarts and the new behavior will have become the new habit.

The exercises are designed to cluster in the following ways:...

1. The "Keep at it" habit addresses the issues in the exercise above for habits 1,2, and 3. The keep at it habit helps you stay on task just a few more minutes.
2. The "What am I missing?" habit addresses 4, 7, 8, 9, and 10. By being on the lookout for what we are missing we expand our criticality and potential for transference.
3. The "Tightening" habit is helpful in areas 5, 6, 7, and 13. There is always room for growth in precision.
4. The "It's more than it seems" habit helps us overcome conformational bias. Opening our eyes to others' points of view and seeing from new angles builds cognitive flexibility.
5. The habit of "Taking big and small risks" helps us overcome the challenges in 15 and embrace change.
6. The "Taking yourself along and building connections" habit addresses 16 and is both foundational to becoming a reflective practitioner and building your new social network.

Exercise #1: The "Keep at it" or Focus Habit. To build this habit you need a baseline against which to measure your success. As an example, if you want to increase the amount of time on which you focus your attention on your graduate work prior to getting up to get a cup of coffee, or being distracted by social media, you need to know your current pattern. It may seem tempting to push a little harder when you start a habit and to give yourself a false baseline. This can set us up for disappointment later, so do what you can, to honestly measure where you are now. Then proceed to the following steps.

1. On an average day, and in an average mood, notice the time when you start your work.
2. Whenever you first notice a distraction, mark down that time as well, whether or not you give into it.
3. Proceed with your work and continue writing down times when you notice the tendency to think about distractions, until such a time as you give in and actually change your behavior away from your focus. This has established your baseline.
4. Now open or invest in a timer. You might look into the Pomodoro technique and the many web tools that support it. Pomodoro is handy because it measures your time on task gives you regular breaks.
5. Set the Pomodoro timer for 15 minutes longer than your baseline measurement. As an example, if you started to become distracted after 25 minutes, you would set your timer for 40.
6. Start your timer when you start your work, and do not let yourself give into more than a momentary fleeting thought until the timer goes off. Should you notice yourself becoming distracted prior to that, remind yourself you only must wait until the timer goes off.
7. Continue as a practice until you habitually work for an hour or more without giving in to distraction.

By delaying your distractions, and slowly but incrementally extending the amount of time before you give into them, you will build your focus habit.

Exercise #2: the "What am I missing?" or "Be on the lookout" habit. This habit helps you build consciousness about what you are not seeing at any given time. It starts with making a game out of noticing what has been previously unseen. You can then extend this habit anytime you think about it throughout your life.

1. Go into a room, sit down in a chair, someplace where you are comfortable and the setting feels familiar.

2. Close your eyes, and count to 25 slowly, focusing on your breathing – the object here is to quiet your mental chatter.
3. Open your eyes and look around. Try to find three to five items or nuances of experience of which you were not previously conscious prior to opening your eyes. As an example, how is the light playing off the wall? Or, what new bit of clutter had you not previously seen?
4. Don't judge, just notice and count the number of new insights you have.
5. Repeat the step of closing your eyes, counting, and then opening your eyes and finding new objects, three to four times during your day. Make a game of finding what you are not seeing, anytime you have a moment to consider.
6. For variation play the same game with what you are not seeing in a common situation such as family dinner. Perhaps you close your eyes for a moment and then open them noticing how your children are eating, who is paying attention or not, what is going on around you. In this new way.
7. Another extension would be to play the game during class, noticing things about people or the professor that you had not seen before.

Exercise #3: "Tightening it up". This exercise is built on the idea that no matter who you are there is always something you can do to tighten. A word of caution, this exercise should not be indulged to the point where you feel guilty about things that you are not doing. Do not overlay the tightening it up with guilt.

1. Step one set your Pomodoro timer again. This exercise focuses on the time in between your scheduled sessions. As an example, if your timer is set at 40 minutes on focused time and 10 minutes off increase the 10 minutes off to 12 or 15.
2. After every focused session use the extra 2 to 5 minutes to do something that tightens up your environment. Examples might include reorganizing a few things on your desk, picking up a few dishes in the kitchen, or if you're on campus taking care of a few emails, or spending a few minutes revising the section you just wrote prior to going onto the next.

3. Another word of caution, you should go back to your main task as soon as you accomplish one small tighten. Over time you'll see how these small steps add up to big changes, but you lose the point if you try to do them all at once.

Depending on the particular challenge that you are using this exercise to address will determine how you use your extra minutes. As an example, if you're working on accuracy then you spend your time ensuring that something you just wrote is precisely correct. You might do this for clarity as well. If you are working on communicating, then you would spend the extra time figuring out who or what exactly you want to say. On a mundane level, if you feel overwhelmed by all you have to do, then spending the time first boxing up clutter and then, one by one, finding a new home for it, will help enormously.

Exercise #4: "Its more than it seems". This exercise increases your ability to transfer one idea to other situations and overall increase how widely you apply your ideas and whether they focus inward or outward.

- Continue in a situation where you feel a little stuck until you have gone through all your normal steps of addressing it. At that time close your eyes and count slowly to 25. The purpose of this is to wipe your mental slate clean, so you must concentrate on the numbers as you count.
- Open your eyes and ask yourself…
- What is there about this situation that I am missing? If nothing comes to mind, take out a piece of paper and write down the first few thoughts you have, whether or not you judge them to be appropriate or accurate to the situation.
- Close your eyes, count again, wipe your mental screen and this time when you open your eyes ask yourself, "What other situation have I seen or do I have in my life from which I can transfer something of clarity here?"
- Close your eyes, count again, wipe your mental screen, open your eyes and ask, "What is there in my skills and previous experience which I can apply here that I might not have thought of before now?"

The purpose of this exercise is to allow for a greater communication between your inner wisdom and outer reality. You need to take the breaths and the time to wipe your mental slate clean for that inner voice to be heard. Your ability to listen to that voice will increase with time. Eventually it becomes easy to communicate with your inner wisdom and apply those ideas creatively to any situation.

Exercise #5: "Taking big and small risks". What you consider a risk will be dependent upon your previous history with risk-taking and on decisions you have made about your own personal safety. Therefore, where you are on this continuum will determine the specifics from which you start this exercise.

1. Change the way you do something small, perhaps the hand you use while brushing your teeth. Start a motion like going up stairs, with the opposite foot. Stop yourself saying something you would always say, take a breath, and say something slightly different. Remember, only you will know that you are messing with your normal way of doing things, it won't be obvious to others, so you can make it a game. Notice how these small changes feel.
2. Write a post-it note and put "take risks" or "embrace change" on your computer screen and other places around your house.
3. Increase your risk-taking to situations that do not have defined outcomes. These might include being bold about what you say to others, or wearing bright colors so that you are more noticeable, or doing anything you suspect that may draw uncomfortable notice. This gives you a chance to work through any tendency you have to feel slightly uncomfortable about others' reactions.
4. Write down what happens and give yourself a moment to reflect on your feelings about those situations. Proceed over time until the small bold steps no longer frighten you.
5. Take a bolder step. You are ready now to try something that would've been completely impossible before you started this exercise.

Being able to comfortably take risks should proceed over a period of time. I have found that writing myself post-it notes and putting them up reminds me to take these exercise time-outs. Eventually telling my friends I'm working on a new skill and asking them to check in on how it is going works, or writing about it myself regularly through journals, etc. It is important to set up little reminders to keep my progression along a bigger trajectory on the positive side of skill development.

Exercise #6: "Taking yourself along" or "Building connections". This exercise addresses the importance of humor and caring, bringing our humanity into everything we do. You may find that the academic environment, because of the natural tendency to focus so much on mental activity, is less interconnected than other areas of your life. The purpose is to ensure that the academic environment contains all the human supports that you would wish for.

1. Spend the day not changing any outward behavior on campus but noticing any and all situations which you might find as humorous or ironic.
2. Write down what you see. Consider humor and irony in your academic world as it compares to other parts of your life. Are you lighthearted on campus? Why or why not?
3. Consider where your behavior might bring humor, humanity or irony to a situation. Practice on small situations where people may not know you personally such as the person working at the bookstore or cafeteria, your librarians, the security man at the door, etc. How might you enliven their lives and bring a smile to their faces, bringing a sense of humor or humanity into your university life?
4. Next, after a few days, consider how to enliven the humanity in your classrooms, with your professors, with your committee members or advisors.

Remember it is your responsibility to bring yourself and your own humanity into any environment. Knowing people's names, sharing a smile, even something as simple as inquiring about their children or sharing stories related to the weather, are all ways in which to ensure you bring yourself along.

Resourcefulness

The king of all skills for thriving is resourcefulness. I was reminded of this by a student in one of our groups. She commented that she had noticed the difference between moving ahead and getting stuck was others propensity to either accept their "bad" experience or keep looking until they found a solution that helped them past the blocks they faced.

Likely you, as someone who reached out towards a book looking for the hidden secrets of graduate life, are a resourceful person. Keep at it! Don't give up and never believe you must simply cave in and quit, or worse yet, accept a situation that you find intolerable. While this does not give you license to stubbornly continue your graduate path without compromise, it does remind you that there are many ways to approach any situation. You need to keep finding resources until you can see your way clear to a place that keeps you safe as you move forward in your graduate work, no matter the difficulties you face.

Chapter Six

Transferrable Attitudinal Skills for Graduate School and Your Next Job

As work changes, the human experience of life changes with it, never more than right now. What makes our current times different? To understand why it is important to upgrade your attitudinal skills in order to thrive through this next bit of evolutionary change, it's useful to look at the outcome of similar shifts in the past. First, steam mechanization changed the way work was done, removing it from always relying on man's muscles, to machines. The second shift occurred because of electricity, increasing mass production causing the way people worked to transform. This resulted in large numbers of people moving into cities and the urban landscape developed. Just in the last few decades computers changed the way knowledge was transferred resulting in changes across all types of human communication. Currently all those changes converge as mechanization strips jobs, artificial intelligence changes the way we interact with our environments, smart technologies change our physical spaces, biotechnologies change what we depend on for life. The current pace of change outstrips what we have faced before, and at the heart of whether these changes are a blessing, or a curse, are human interactions and whether we can provide enough education to adequately upskill workers. (*Zahidi, S., 2020*).

Humans are not hardwired to handle change well as our biological systems evolve slowly. The fourth Industrial Revolution increases divergent possibilities of how we live our lives, causing greater gaps to open between lifestyles and access to services. Smart leadership will do what it can to avoid negative scenarios such as massive unemployment, as we begin to embrace artificial intelligence, data analytics, biotechnology, smart homes and cities, block chain commerce, etc. As you think about the changing environment into which your graduate life propels you, realize that these changes impact economy, business, government, society, and each one of us as individuals. The velocity of the disruption and the acceleration of these innovations are hard to comprehend or to anticipate (*Schwab, 2016*).

This section looks at the attitudinal skills? That the World Economic Forum suggests are required by leaders going forward. I use them as way markers for my personal and professional growth and believe you will find them helpful as well. Included here are emotional intelligence, negotiation, coordinating with others, people management, and service orientation.

Emotional Intelligence

The current level of change requires cross system collaboration across diverse populations and contexts for most types of professionals. These types of environments test humanity's ability to work together. The research and literature on emotional intelligence goes back 25 to 30 years and was largely popularized by Goleman (*1996; Goleman, et al., 2017*). He presented a model with 25 competencies in five clusters. The clusters were: self-awareness, self-regulation, motivation, empathy, and social skills. Each included subcategories and competencies but the reader can see just from this overview that all of them are required in any collaborative environment.

While it is possible for people with a finite set of highly specialized skills to do well in the world without emotional intelligence, it requires that they are so advanced that people overlook the challenges of working with them. For most of us being that advanced would be an impossible task. Therefore, a distinct difference between thriving and failure can be our level of emotional intelligence.

For leadership, emotional intelligence becomes critical. A leader needs to be able to sense and address other people's feelings, moods and emotions, contributing to effective development of organizations. Four aspects of emotional intelligence come to play here: how you appraise and express emotion, how you use it to enhance your cognitive processes, the role of emotion in how you make decisions and how you personally manage your own emotions when dealing with others..

When mastered, emotional intelligence contributes to effective leadership in five ways; it helps you:

1. Work with others to establish mutual goals and objectives.

2. Lead teams past daily hurdles.
3. Build and encourage enthusiasm in others.
4. Embrace cognitive flexibility and help others to do so as well.
5. Stay resilient through challenging times.

Emotional intelligence can be an aid to our own mental health. The therapeutic nurse, as an example carries a risk of burnout because of the prolonged or intense relationship with ill patients. Research found that those who applied emotional intelligence to their own lives were better at applying self-care when needed and therefore had better long-term outcomes (*McQueen, 2004*).

That same protection through self-care is widely necessary, as jobs change – whether cancelled or created - requiring new skills. Training can help people reinvent their future, but emotional intelligence is needed to maneuver through reorganization of corporations, maintain a positive flow of work in the face of disruption, build depleted morale, etc. The true potential of emotional intelligence is to allow all of us to work to become more interconnected rather than less, as a result of technology.

General steps. Rather than a specific exercise, emotional intelligence being such a large process, this section closes with five general steps you can incorporate in your life which will slowly but consistently build your emotional intelligence quota.

- **Step one** – connect with the world, discover large challenges and involve yourself in them in some way. Work to feel like you're part of a bigger picture, not just focused on your everyday life. This might include volunteering at a homeless shelter or food bank, etc.
- **Step 2** -take 100% responsibility for the consequences of your actions. This includes apologizing and making amends, working to be kind and humble, and acting out of a high ethical standard.
- **Step 3** – develop strong listening skills. Imagine other people as though you loved and cared for them, how would you wish all of the people that you do love and care for to be treated? Treat everyone in that manner. Compassion counts.

- **Step 4** -when interacting with people very different from yourself, work to understand what life must be like through their eyes and experiences. Ask questions, rather than judge.
- **Step 5** – reach out, be giving, be grateful. This can be towards people who are less advantaged than yourself, or others that you interact with daily and may take for granted, be your best human self.

There are number of ways you can build emotional intelligence in graduate school. Peer review and embracing group assignments allow you to be in communication with others and involved in activities where understanding your emotional effect as well as your cognitive abilities are important. Personally, and privately, you can embrace meditation as a way to not only calm your own daily stress, but to appreciate the challenges of life as experienced by others. Reflective practice, journaling, etc. will help you track your efforts as you learn to watch facial expressions and then respond by checking out whether or not what you thought you saw was what the other person was in fact experiencing. Try hanging out with people that make you a little uncomfortable, learning to understand rather than judge.

Video resources.

- **Emotional intelligence, a video:** https://pd.education/job-prep-video-snippets/video/150-emotional-intelligence.html
- **Making positive progress, utilize your brain emotional networks:** https://pd.education/job-prep-video-snippets/video/141-making-positive-progress-utilize-your-brain-emotional-networks.html

Negotiation

There are two types of negotiation: distributive and integrative. Distributive negotiation is when you want one thing, as in the best price when you're selling your house, as you will not have a relationship with that person afterwards, so you do what you can to get the best for yourself. The second type of negotiation is integrative. This is when you will have an ongoing relationship, or what you do now will have ongoing repercussions past this particular moment. Imagine a divorce handled by both parties in a distributive manner, complete with high-cost lawyers, and severe property disagreements. How well does that work for them in the long run? This is an example of an integrative negotiation handled in a distributive manner.

Change requires negotiation, as it is seldom true that we can just simply implement our ideas without involving others. When looking at the converging amount of change in the world, we can only imagine what this will mean to our economic lives, our businesses, the way we interact with our governments, how our society and cultures will change with each generation and what all of this means to our friends and families. There will be growth and diminishment of people's economy as employment changes and new skills as well as the nature of work change.

Businesses will be impacted on all levels. We will be required to negotiate customers' expectations, their ability to work with data enabled products, and, as researchers, we will be required to collaborate globally and across markets. Nothing will be static. Not even our governments, so it will require us to negotiate how we interact with our public institutions. To the extent that as academics we may be employed by public institutions this change could change everything from the standards of what is taught to how it is delivered, where, and to whom. No longer do we have the time to study a specific issue and create a response, when the world is changing this fast we tend to develop an "always in beta" stance, rolling out solutions before we have a chance to study their consequences. Because people change slowly compared to technology, there will be a wider and wider spectrum of understanding, with many levels of personal realities conflicting. The role of education in the world will shift (*Schwab & Davis, 2018*).

The convergence of these dynamics has some people worried. What we want to avoid is developing a "me centered" society. We might well see new sources of mistrust, inequality, embedded bias, and scaling tensions. Positive potentials, if managed well, will include higher levels of employment, greater personal satisfaction as work-life balance shifts, and a global social environment. Critical policy questions requiring negotiation include: a) how governments will manage these transitions and the costs that are associated with them; b) how citizens' rights will be protected; c) how to best manage increasing levels of data security and privacy while still allowing people the greatest possible flexibility (*Schwab, 2016; Schwab & Davis, 2018*).

Habits of mind in line with negotiation skills. What personal habits should you consider building to prepare you for negotiation, and interdependent living? Covey, (1989, 2003, 2016), outlines them as: a) develop a win-win attitude; b) seek first to understand before being understood; and, c) synergize with others, building, rather than directing. Once again, your personal awareness is key, as each requires that you know yourself and what you are willing to compromise, and, when you will not accept a compromise, why not? By being creative and pulling in new ideas, you will be able to suggest an option for mutual gain where you may not have seen one originally.

Negotiation may require full disclosure. It can be helpful to those you work with to understand motivations as well as facts. This may require more vulnerability on your part than you are comfortable with at first. You can start whenever you need to negotiate with classmates, or your committee, by telling them the full story as to why you need or are suggesting a course of action on their part.

Remember that people are not the problem. When insecure, it is easy to project negative judgments onto the other as though "they" are the problem. A graduate example is that during review it is easier to imagine "they" don't understand rather than "I" didn't say that well. Reframing to consider the others' interests and perspectives help our work develop.

Exercise one: Be prepared. The following eight groups of questions help you prepare for negotiation.

1. In order to understand everyone else's goals as well as your own, ask, "What are you trying to achieve during the negotiation?" and "What do you think the other person's goals are?"
2. In order to prepare for compromise to build consensus, ask yourself, "What are you willing to trade?" "What might you be able to give away or let go of?" and, finally, "What do you expect the other person to offer you?"

3. In order to investigate alternatives in case negotiation breaks down, ask yourself, "What if you can't achieve your goals?" "What would be your best alternative?" Know your options.

4. Because negotiation relies on relationship, do your homework. Know how negotiations with this other party have worked out in the past. Ask yourself, "What kind of relationship do you expect or want to have with them in the future?"

5. Ask yourself, "Are there precedents at work here?" Investigate other similar situations and what the intended and unintended consequences were in those cases. Based on those and your current understanding of the situation you face, what seems the most likely outcome?

6. In order to fully prepare for consequences, ask yourself, "Is this one or part of many small negotiations?" "Will this issue keep coming back?" "What do you need and what does the other party stand to lose or gain? and "Can you both have everything you want if developed over a period of time?"

7. Look into the dynamic of power, ask yourself, "Who holds the power?" "How will this affect the negotiation?"

8. Consider possible scenarios given all of your answers to the previous seven points. What do you now consider to be a fair outcome?

Exercise two: Once prepared, plan your strategy.

	Importance of Ongoing Relationship	
Importance of Outcome	High / Low = Accommodation	High / High = Collaborate
	Low / Low = Avoid or dictate	Low / High = Compete

Figure 1: Negotiation Matrix of Power and Outcome

The 2 x 2 matrix above is useful when considering your relative power in the negotiation and how much accommodation you may be facing.

High-Low: When it is important to you to maintain the relationship but this particular negotiation doesn't matter, you will accommodate to them.

High-High. If the relationship is high but the outcome is high as well then you need to push towards a collaborative solution.

Low-Low: If the relationship is low and you don't really care about the person, probably you'll just avoid the situation, or if you can't, you'll try to dictate the outcome.

Low-High: If the relationship is low and yet the outcome is high you may find yourself just competing rather than negotiating, as in the earlier example of selling your house.

Once you understand your particular position within this negotiation consider the following and enact as appropriate.

1. Test out their stance with them. Question what you are assuming are their motivations. Why are they thinking feeling or behaving this way? I like the phrase, "What I hear you saying is...."

2. Be aware of your values and be transparent about them to others. Share your position whether it aligns with theirs or not. "From my point of view, (and I suspect it does not match yours)"

3. Expand the pie. In other words, consider the bigger picture and make that the important outcome. Then you will find it easier to negotiate the small points. "If we expand this conversation, maybe we can agree that the greater good might be...."

4. Brainstorm new solutions in a collaborative environment. Others who are different from you may see options you don't. "What ideas do others here have that I may be missing?"

5. Trade favors. What can you give up? What do you want them to give up? "I see we are at an impasse but maybe compromise on both sides can get us past this. I see that I can bend...."

6. Match outcomes. One to one, what did you get as a positive and what did they receive that they wanted? Keep those considerations on the table as you come to stickier conversations. "I appreciate that you compromised on XXXX. Would it help us find a solution if YYY?"

7. When you do not feel you can accommodate, see if there is another way forward. For instance, the essence of graduate defense is to listen, consider and then come back with examples from literature of others who have done it your way. Could that strategy work in this situation you are facing now?

Video resources.

- **Negotiation, a video:** https://pd.education/job-prep-video-snippets/video/153-negotiation.html
- **Career transference 201: 10 Skills needed in work and how to ensure you have them:** https://pd.education/job-prep-video-snippets/video/53-career-transference-201-10-skills-needed-in-work-and-how-to-ensure-you-have-them.html

Coordinating with Others

As recently as a decade ago, many jobs required far less coordination with others than they do now. The trend towards coordination of efforts is escalating and will continue, not only at a local level but globally and in a virtual environment. Each has its own peculiarities to consider.

Take for instance coordination of patient care during confinement in a hospital. It used to be that specific practitioners came in and worked with the patient and the only commonality was the patient's experience and their records. Now generalists practice and working in teams with care coordination has become a norm. This requires improved communication among clinicians with the team approach including integration of patients and family members as partners. An "all stakeholders approach" requires that data-driven practices are transparent, and all medical informants have access to, and input on, those data. Holistic care has the possibility to provide astonishing levels of care but also requires more effort because of the effort to coordinate (*Zamanzadeh, V. et al., 2015*).

Gone are the days of experts ruling the stage. As long ago as 1999, Durfee pointed out that even in the mechanical world, agents who know much are subjected to cockiness, confusion, paralysis, and other unpleasant statements. An individual agent committed to their own mission may have a tendency to either drive it through or, if they have power, assign what they want to the group. This analogous look at coordination suggests that everyone can gain more by giving up what they know and merging efforts and forward movement toward their goal.

The basics. No one will be willing to coordinate under all circumstances. The person responsible for coordinating the effort needs to understand each individual position and provide some flexibility of requirement, depending upon the circumstances. Not one size will fit all, every actor needs to have the freedom to draft their own course through a coordinated effort.

It is not as simple as, "Just communicate more." Too much information could be as bad as too little. Easy coordination requires enough information to act on but not so much as to confuse the issues. Perhaps you have been involved in a conversation where one person's point of view droned on beyond everyone else's understanding. This would be an example where it becomes critical to act when an action is needed, rather than listen completely to the non-significant standards or informants.

Routines may need to be established that ensure both proper communication and pragmatic outcomes are achievable. Teams need to keep their focus on getting results. Is your scientific research being done for a particular client? Then, as an example, coordinating the efforts must keep the satisfaction of that grant provider in mind.

When working in an innovative environment extra care needs to be taken because external unknowns cannot be predicted. In industry employing agile development, frequent communications, testing at the pre-beta level, ensure a greater likelihood of success rather than failure. As Dorner (1998) found, the more complex the situation the more likely that failure will follow unless leaders constantly watch for unintended outcomes.

Practical coordination requires someone takes the role of the person who keeps track of what is going on, continually highlights and measures outcomes against the goals, and takes care of tracking the emotional content and reactions as well as the physical ones. The following discussion shows you how to employ these basics in a mentor/supervisor – graduate student negotiation.

Exercise: Negotiating with your advisor or supervisor. This exercise considers the basics described above in backwards order. Some may come up against barriers within your university –investigate before taking action.

1. In a graduate student/supervisor negotiation it is expected that the student will take the roleof keeping track of the timeline. This requires that after a meeting with part of your committee it is advisable to send notes on what occurred to everyone, including a calendar of expected future events, adjusted according to the newest information.

2. Many committee members may not be interested in reading partial drafts. How then can a student meet the innovative criteria to test pre-beta (pre full-draft stage)? Suggested possibilities include joining a graduate writing group, finding a coach or outside reader who goes over your work as you write it making suggestions, etc.

3. Establishing both work and communication routines and have them agreed upon by all stakeholders can be important. If you complete a draft by a due date, you need to negotiate how long the supervisor will take before reviewing and getting comments back to you. Know whether they want to see each chapter when it is in solid draft or only after another's review?

4. How much information to share about the complications in your life relative to your graduate work is necessary so that your committee can understand your circumstances and adjust appropriately? If and when you need to ask for an extension due to personal circumstances, do they know you well enough that they will not see this as a student taking advantage? Only you can decide the proper answers here given your circumstances, but some professors may coordinate what they do more willingly when they know more about your personal circumstance.

5. Have you spoken with other students who have had these professors on their committees? Every circumstance is different but knowing how they reacted in the past may help.

With this, and assuming you have worked all the exercises for the attitudinal skills, you have built a strong set of habits and routine behaviors. You have honed your emotional intelligence and should be better at reading human situations correctly. You have learned to negotiate and, once you understand the situation, you can help it move in the direction that you desire. Being able to coordinate work with others will make you an asset to any team. These three skills package together nicely for any work environment, academic or industry. But what if you work with people who have problematic personality traits?

Video Resource.

- **Coordinating with others:** https://pd.education/job-prep-video-snippets/video/53-career-transference-201-10-skills-needed-in-work-and-how-to-ensure-you-have-them.html
- **Career transference 201: 10 Skills needed in work and how to ensure you have them:** https://pd.education/job-prep-video-snippets/video/53-career-transference-201-10-skills-needed-in-work-and-how-to-ensure-you-have-them.html

People Management

People management conjures up pictures of people in middle or upper management positions who are responsible for the work produced by others. This is not the only application of people management skills. At the basic level, mothers and fathers manage children and families daily. Graduate students manage their graduation process and thus the professorial team that supports them to continue to move on. No matter where you are in the graduate process people management skills may be important.

It may be optimistic to say, "Good management is the art of making problems so interesting and their solution so constructive that everyone wants to get to work and deal with them" (*Hawkens, ND as quoted by Adevey, 2013*). Yet, at its core, people management is helping everyone see how the activities they are engaged in are going in a positive direction so that they too can experience a lift from doing that work. For a graduate student, this is having a project and a life path that engages their committees at more than the norm for a student-professor relationship.

The basics. The steps of people management are applicable whether managing from the bottom (as in graduate life) or the top. First, establish an effective work climate; second, implement rigorous practices or disciplines; third, capitalize on and grow individual talent; fourth, build effective team structures within work groups; fifth, implement broad-based people management strategies. The examples below take these five steps through two practical discussions. The first looks at a graduate student managing a team of professors who will be their committee during their final thesis, and the second looks at parents managing children.

As a graduate student you are not in control of any of the aspects of these five levels but can influence situations in a positive direction. Establishing an effective work climate, entails regular communication with professors, setting timelines. delivering writing as expected and having a positive upbeat attitude whenever you meet. These will encourage everyone you work with to see your research and writing moving forward, taking the pressure off of them as to whether or not you will be a drag on their workload and making you seem a pleasant person with whom to work.

What does it look like in graduate school to implement rigorous people management practices? It means that you stay in touch. As an example, you ask for and expect the people around you to follow the schedule mutually decided upon. You discuss with others that that you intend to have chapters one, two and three finished by a certain time. Then you ask, "How does that fit with the professor's schedule? Will they be able to turn it around? If that timing works, how long do they anticipate before you can expect a response? Then it's perfectly legitimate that should these expectations not be met; you can feel comfortable asking for the response. As a graduate student you need to manage this carefully and not come across as arrogant or pushy, but adults can expect to work with other adults in a regular fashion. Establishing that level of conversation will be helpful. The final chapter in this book has sections pertaining to when these expectations aren't met.

You will want to capitalize on the individual talents of your committee. Each professor has skills you will find helpful, but none of them will give you everything you need. Some types of support are personal, some of them rigorously academic, etc. Apply emotional intelligence to understand who is good for what kind of support, then capitalize on that by working one-on-one. Remember professors are resources but it is your responsibility to employ their suggestions. Never become a drain.

Your responsibility to build an effective support team includes not just those that you are immediately involved with. Always include your graduate school office, your advisors, mental health workers, nurses, librarians etc. as part of your support team. These individuals may have more time or have a broader range of supports to offer.

How does the fifth, and final, step in people management, to implement broad-based strategies for the future, equate to graduate school? As mentioned elsewhere in this book, networks are the important way to move forward in any career. You build those networks one person at a time through partaking in different experiences. A good place to start is by taking advantage of professional development opportunities on your campus. Be friendly, offer support to others when you see a need, and become familiar with others so you can ask for the support later if you need it.

As you take on managing people, you will have to find your own way as to what works. However, two clusters of practices will be significant for you to build a high performing team: first, acquire and develop the right people, then design the work to include flexibility and variety so everyone enjoys the process. These skills can be developed during class projects. The next time you're invited by your professor to work as a group, consider who you want to work with not from who you like but for those whose diversity will be an asset in helping you get the job done. And then use your energy to help the group design the work so that no one feels overburdened or given a task they don't really want to do. Be able to use your negotiation skills to make sure that people are happy with the design so that the project can move forward without stress. These will make great interview stories when applying for your next job.

In closing the section on people management, it's important to remember that as soon as you see others as wrong, impossible, hard to deal with, etc., you are already on the slippery slope towards failure. The only outlook that works overtime is that all human beings are just doing the best we can. When others are argumentative, stressed, less than easy to deal with, there are extenuating circumstances over and above this moment. The more we understand each other's personal circumstances, the more we can drill through the momentary trouble and build the relationships that allow us to work productively.

Common difficulties. Rather than conclude with an exercise, this section ends with a list of the common difficulties in working with others. Use it when you are working with someone whose personality gets in the way of your productivity.

Overconfident. When a person oversteps their obvious abilities and skills, the solution may be to quietly gather data about where their outputs were not what they led others to expect. Meet with them privately and show that you believe in their promise, if not their performance, at the moment. Encourage them to tone down on what they say in order to build others' trust.

Low ambition or not motivated to do the work. This is difficult because there can be so many reasons a person is not motivated; some may be clinical or embedded personality issues. Before you can motivate, you must know the person well enough to understand what incentive will work. If you can, build their personal trust through being truthful, and then bluntly ask for change.

Annoying or persistently irritating. This trait may reflect that the person is facing a change they did not expect or do not like. It's important to find the person's motivation points and ignite those, while being upfront about how irritating and annoying it is to others when they slow down the work process. Listening to their complaints and reflecting back that you heard them is always the first step.

Controlling or micromanaging. People who have to control every part of every task may be driven by insecurity. Keep clear boundaries on what you have said you will do, what is your responsibility, and when is the right time to hear critique and aid efficiencies. Be clear that it delays the work to have each task looked at separately. This is a good team discussion so the group can set boundaries for everyone.

Unsociable. Are these group members introverts, loners, or do they just hate the process? Seek to understand and then build on their strengths and motivate them to join in if that is what's truly required.

Sometimes a quieter introverted group member can successfully work on their own, as long as their solitary behavior does not negatively impact others' work. Allow for different structures within required human interaction.

Volatile, passionate or perfectionists. These people monopolize our time and may be dangerous and negative in any situation depending on the level of volatility. Other team members naturally keep a distance from these people which may aggravate the situation. As a team leader, your ability to keep calm and maintain some distance through questioning, rather than engaging behaviors, is key. Help them understand when they are having a negative impact on the outcome of the group. Volatility can often be addressed using more formal performance agreements.

Dominant, always wanting to be in control. These need people to challenge them, to play off of their good traits in a manner that is fearless. Someone who is calm under stress can be direct and assertive, encourage teamwork, and calm a dominant person down to help them be part of the team. These people often can be positive influences on output. You do not want to clip their wings, just chart a path where they can shine and yet not overshadow others.

Defensive. At their core, these people are afraid. Their behavior irritates and when others snap at them it exacerbates the challenge. A team leader should not play into that cycle, but rather soothe and then correct.

Extremely sensitive. These people may feel as though they are victims. Discussing their sensitivity with them and helping them set up boundaries can encourage team process. Give them more space than you would others. Leave them alone to get their work done.

Arrogant, rude, abrupt. Here the challenge is not only the personality, but also an inability to listen or follow directions. People management requires that your goal be to help them change that to self-confidence which is the other side of the same coin. Consider what they do well. Praise them for it just before you point out the things that cause frustrations. This can help balance arrogance. Over time, this first positive-then-negative approach may transform a personality disorder to a positive self-confidence.

Grumpy. People who are grumpy may be jostled out of their grumpiness through a happy environment where humor is not attacking but cajoles them to become more positive. Work to make them smile, and then distract them from their own grumpiness.

Gifted and intense. Often complex, with a lot of drive, these people may not always the easy to work with. Gifted people are frequently emotionally sensitive so always be benevolent and supportive and hold their performance to agreed-upon standards. These people can become your shining stars, so you'll want to encourage disclosure of what they feel is limiting or threatening. Verbalization can help cut back on their intensity.

What is it like, being a person managing other people? It is challenging and takes a lot of time, but you can get so much more done that in the end it should be worth the trouble. Whether you are their boss or their teammate the same strategies apply: 1) find commonality with others; 2) listen to and understand their points of view; 3) be honest and forthright; and 4) set boundaries on the situation in order to develop a mutually agreed-upon path.

Critique requires self-awareness. Ask yourself how much of the situation is you, rather than them. Self-regulation is the key to avoid over-reaction. If you understand your own motivations, you can set your personality aside in order to confront a situation from a neutral position. You need to have empathy to understand possible reactions and help the other person respond well to what could be construed as criticism. In order to do this well, strong social skills are needed, which take a lifetime to develop. Graduate school can be an excellent opportunity to hone these individual skills as you work in rather intimate settings with people who are not well known to you.

Video resource.

- **People Management skills transferable from graduate work:** https://pd.education/wellness-video-snippets/video/41-managing-graduate-school-using-project-management-practices.html

Service Orientation

Having a service orientation to your life, your work, how you interact with other people, is a basic human value, although it is also something that you can develop. Mahatma Gandhi is quoted as saying that "the best way to find yourself is to lose yourself in the service of others" (*as quoted by Din, 2010*). But giving real service is something that requires you to engage your emotional intelligence so that what you propose is appropriate and pleasurable to the situation or people to whom it is offered. As Covey reminds us, having our values and wanting to do well by other people grounds us in a life that is fulfilling and one that makes your work highly effective (2003).

Service may be, but is not necessarily, without profit. Service can be complex as in developing and running a program for hundreds of people, or as simple as daily exchanges that cause a smile and share humanity. The popular phrase is to think globally and act locally, as our service in a small way is also beneficial to our world. People engaged in graduate school might find that the easiest service is to be teaching other people to understand things that they may not yet know or have access to. A service orientation comes from a disposition to be helpful, thoughtful, considerate, and cooperative (*Rubin, et al., 1984 page 167*) and these traits also naturally coincide with the best teammates and /or teachers.

When considering current levels of innovation and change, several kinds of service come to mind. As people change jobs, they will need new skills. As people have to use machines, they will need training. As people face their fear of what they will be able to do next, they will need encouragement. As people see change around them and become frightened, they need to be taught ethics and values to ensure the change results in a healthier world. Since graduate students are often employed in teaching, you may have an opportunity, to be a positive impact in all of these situations.

Every industry is in the midst of change and a service orientation propels you to step in when you see negative consequences evolving around you. For example, in business if you see environmental decay, poor worker morale, or disengagement of employees from families, services are required. When scientific breakthroughs or data intelligence are misused, and you see destructive or intrusive consequences you might explain and then point out to others the dangers in the current environment. Even in the leisure industry you might see changes that cause an increase in accidents or lack of awareness. In education it might be that institutions are not doing all they can to meet the needs of students and your voice can help propel positive change. Whatever the circumstance, it is morally incumbent on us all to do what we can.

Considerations. The following list of ideas to consider may help you build or increase your natural service orientation.

1.   Think of some small thing that is helpful to others and then put it into action. Note the results and build on them. You will not be Mother Teresa overnight.
2.   Spend time meditating, contemplating, praying, or engaging in reflective practice. Taking time out allows you to enlarge your awareness and bring that back to service you can provide.
3.   Offer help. Volunteer your skills to organizations that need helping hands.
4.   When you offer service and it is declined don't be dismayed. Accepting help is not easy for people.
5.   If you are in a management or leadership position, see if you can work on the overall climate of those around you to increase service everywhere.
6.   Once service is part of a culture, work to ensure that people have enough power to act independently and do what they think needs to be done.

Video resource.

- **Service orientation:** https://pd.education/job-prep-video-snippets/video/156-service-orientation.html
- **Career transference 201: 10 Skills needed in work and how to ensure you have them:** https://pd.education/job-prep-video-snippets/video/53-career-transference-201-10-skills-needed-in-work-and-how-to-ensure-you-have-them.html

To Wrap this Up

Bringing our wholeness, our humanity along as we grow is an endeavor that continues right up until the time we die if we are lucky. Those of us with academic training and deep cognitive skills are doubly lucky because we are more likely to see and understand the changes we go through and make cognitively driven adjustments as desired. This chapter bridged those gaps – between the cognitive and the spirit, between academia and the totality of our lives as human beings. I hope it also offered useful exercises and ideas that you may have chosen to implement right away.

Whichever the challenge, cognitive, as in Chapter One, or attitudinal as in this chapter, sometimes situations in graduate school can go very wrong. Those situations and clues as to where you might go for help will be covered in Chapter Seven.

Chapter Seven

Troubled Waters in Graduate School?
In an Ideal World... an Introduction

The solutions for many of the issues raised in this chapter depend on having skills covered in detail throughout this book, both the cognitive, attitudinal and the metacognitive. This chapter addresses the challenges that cause students to feel desperate and is not for everyone. Seriously troubled waters are defined as those when you are at risk of disengagement, or you feel seriously insecure, anxious, or depressed.

Graduate school is meant to be a mountain climb, even one as serious as Mount Everest, but, just like Mount Everest, many people have done it before you. There are great guides, and well-known strategies. While not making a positive outcome is guaranteed, they make it within the realm of tolerance for anyone who is resilient and willing to keep learning and keep persisting. If you have tried those and still want to throw in the towel, then read on.

There are a series of challenges that are serious and demand immediate attention. Should you ever feel this insecure, you absolutely must reach out for help. Those challenges are briefly discussed here. They include bullying or noncommunicative committees, anxiety and depression, and any challenges that put your life at risk such as food, shelter, or other physical insecurities.

Underlying this entire chapter is one theme. Your graduate school team is the main advocate, or place to start whenever your attachment to your graduate work begins to break down. Recently, at a Council of Graduate School's meeting, a Dean discussed a challenge where one of the graduate students ended up in litigation between the student and her University, the point was that she did not know the entire situation was going on until it got to legal counsel. Many of you are mostly attached to your program, what you are learning, finishing your research, etc. and don't spend much time considering the wider picture of graduate education at the university. While that is as it should be, it is important to know that your university graduate school is also as committed to your graduate education as your program. Therefore, when you run into challenges with one, the other can provide a different light on your situation and may help you negotiate a different course. In fact, cultivating a relationship early on should be part of your networking goal.

Included in this section is a discussion of graduate processes around the world so that you can see the breadth and width of the choices universities are making and understand where negotiation might be possible. I then move into a discussion of how working with people is a two-sided endeavor and discuss some of the breakdowns from both sides of the table. After drilling into issues of ambiguity, managing expectations, and working with independence, this chapter then moves on to issues of timing, anxiety, legal and ethical rights, and what to do when facing food or housing insecurity.

Different Processes Around the World

Masters and PhD processes at universities around the world are both similar and different to each other. What is similar is a focus on academic thought, criticality, argumentation, and research. What differs slightly from each other are issues of theoretically based scientifically oriented thought and practically based thought, usually teasing out to two streams within a university structure and also known as research degrees or professional degrees. These end in either the PhD or one of many other Doctoral degrees (EdD, DM, DPH, etc). If you review the final documentation from different parts of the world but within the same topical area, they are more similar than different.

Some universities do not offer postgraduate classes, just throwing the student into their final research track without specific topical guidance (this is usual in Europe). The student may enter with an idea or research that is supported by either their supervisor's grants or a company, and they proceed to do the work in the lab while learning the literature. When the research? is over they are expected to write it up and defend a thesis. In the US model, "taught" degrees (as they are referred to around the world) include mandatory classes in the subject as well as research into a topical area. The Master's degree can be a milestone in and to itself or it can be a step along the way to a PhD.

While the processes are not the same around the world, the end results are remarkably similar, yet there are a few differences worthy of attention. In the United States, the culminating event for the Master's degree may be a comprehensive examination, a capstone project or a research thesis. In Europe, if it is its own outcome, it would be more likely to be a dissertation (I thought Europe called them thesis irrespective of level?). At the PhD level, there are differences in terminology used. In the US, you write a dissertation for your PhD and complete with a final defense. In Europe, you write a PhD thesis and complete with a Viva. Around the world, some disciplines are moving away from either, or incorporating a need to publish in journals as part of the journey. I just want to emphasize that no matter your context or requirements, the logic underlying your final work must adhere to standards that will be the same across disciplines.

When we dig past the language, we see other significant, and in one case legal, difference. In the United States, at the doctoral level, it is the norm that the student be required to write three full chapters, the background, literature review, and methodology, which go before the committee for defense of that proposal, for institutional review prior to data collection. This is not the norm in Europe where more likely the student does an extensive literature review, is able to discuss their work and their ideas, has ongoing communication with their committee and then are passed to institutional review and data collection. .

Both procedures are difficult and may contribute to students' work breaking down, but at different times in the process. In the United States students frequently stall out at the proposal stage, with many not making it through to collect data. The reason that the proposal stage is as significant a barrier as it can be considered a somewhat binding contract between yourself and your university (please note case law differs state-to-state). At the point when the student has passed proposal the University can be seen as having taken on a legal obligation to graduate the student as long as their final work meets standard educational criteria, and completes the work as designed in that proposal (there are some caveats on this as you will see in the conclusion to this chapter). This protects the student from committees that change supervisors who retire etc. and later new members demand entirely new tracks of thought and process, which would prohibit timely finishing.

In Europe it is not uncommon for a student to be mostly finished with data collection and perhaps even analysis, only to realize that they do not understand the structure of the final documentation required. I have always called this "retrofitting," as they fit their words about the methodology to what actually happened, rather than to what was designed. In this way it is similar to a final report in the business environment.

In the US, the student may falter on the proposal side of things working very diligently to make it through the peer review process of the review and defense of proposal. It is tough to pull documentation together coherently when you only half understand the intricacies you will learn when you do it. The committee's job is to protect the university from less than rigorous work, as reputations are built on the published work. Sometimes what the committee wants will seem extreme, and perhaps the standard was not properly identified leading into review, so that the back and forth communication may drag.

Many of the challenges of students working on their final documentation are more a challenge of negotiation, cognitive flexibility, complex problem-solving, coordinating with others, and people management. Therefore, I refer you back to those sections of the book that deal with the 10 skills required for all of us to thrive in the fourth Industrial Revolution.

Academic environments have their own peculiarities, but at the end of the day they are people, often with strong egos, who see the world in a particular manner. When we can better understand the reasoning behind the thought that drives the behavior we can negotiate new and different outcomes.

We're all People Here

People are more similar than different. Overarching all of the challenges in graduate school are challenges of humanity. If we accept the idea that most of us have a response to the world that is openhearted and kind and another that is "me" focused (the ego) we see that these two voices or perspectives have very different responses to situations that naturally occur in graduate school.

There are three main ideas which can be seen as being woven throughout the rest of the more specific challenges discussed in this chapter. The first is that there are two sides to every challenge. The second is the requirement for motivation. And the third is how to reengage when you have stopped.

Seeing through the eyes of "the other". When faced with challenges our egos frequently set us up as being on the opposite side of the challenge from "the other." And because we see them as different from ourselves and we righteously see ourselves as being in the right, we then naturally see the other as being wrong. And our ego in our mind work together then to go around and around in circles about how the situation should not be, is not right, they are bad, etc. Frequently, the other person may be having exactly the same but opposite thoughts. Because we know that, we protect our fragile egos and build defensive arguments that exacerbate the spiral of that internal dialog.

When trying to understand the personalities and expectations of the professors you work with, especially those whose background developed during entirely different times and contexts than yours, it is useful to understand that academia is different work and has a different mindset today than it did, even two decades ago. Around the world, the PhD, which is usually the degree required to teach in universities, used to be a much more brutal experience. It is not uncommon for older academics to tell stories of their supervisors picking up their thesis at and throwing it in the trash in front of them. This was in the time when the typed document was the only copy. While not across the board, that level of personal brutality, used to be widely accepted. Also, different disciplines have different expectations of students. Should an older academic gotten their PhD in a time when everyone in the lab was expected to have a sleeping bag there so they could work through the night getting up regularly to manage the experiments, or should they have worked 70 or 80 hours a week for their research, then it is likely they wonder why they can't apply those standards today.

Depending on the amount of hardship that your supervisor personally experienced, they may think those experiences made them more resilient, and they may have crafted ideas about how it makes them a stronger researcher. Therefore, it is natural that they would think that students who are not willing to go through similar experiences are not really worthy of being granted advanced degrees. Even if these attitudes are not personally adhered to, there may be within a university a strong idea that digital native students have less challenge, more leeway, etc. and perhaps they are correct. It is far easier to write a new thesis when word check helps your spelling, when the word processing programs set the document up for you, and when you have an Internet full of ideas at your fingertips.

However, what your professors may not understand is the increased rigor required. Digital tools open a world that is so vast in its knowledge base that it becomes daunting to build coherent arguments when you are just starting. Everyone may feel they are comfortable with juggling more information, but for you, new challenges have replaced the old. If the finite task has become easier with digital services, the mental, philosophical and theoretical tasks have increased in their levels of challenge.

Academic reputation is also different in a world where a never-ending set of examples of expertise, via YouTube and video, are easily streamed. Academics used to have an easier time proving their mental worth via publication and conferences, being big fish in a small pond. With technology the ponds are much bigger, research both good bad and indifferent can be quickly published in a variety of formats, and any given academic has to work very hard to carve out their own personal space. This puts greater stress on professors.

To the extent that you want an academic job, you probably also want help launching your career. This puts another stress on your relationship with your supervisor or chair. Mentorship outside the academy, introducing you to others, becomes more important in the global context. It also puts a requirement on the relationship that needs to be negotiated.

The literature on student supervision discusses the differences that may occur in expectations dependent on whether the student is involved in research that supports their tuition. In the traditional model of Masters and Doctoral work, the student was an apprentice to a wiser and older mentor who supported them in their growth, however when the tuition is supported by research grants or employers, many students will find their supervisor sees them more like an employee, with the supervisor as a project manager (*Holdaway, Debloise, Winchester, 1995*).

Another pivotal area of similarity or difference revolves around what is seen on each side as supportive. The professor may see their role as hands off peer review, thus engendering independence in their students. Students may want the kind old professor, who is always around for a good chat and with whom they tag along to events they would otherwise not be invited to. Better to uncover these differences in opinion and outlook early and with direct negotiation. You are in control when you come armed with literature to guide the discussion, but you need to take that position, know your rights, and negotiate.

Exercise. This negotiation will get your relationships with advisors, supervisors, etc off to a good start. It can also be used if you have to renegotiate along the path to graduation.

1. As you are assigned or working with a particular person in order to finish either your masters capstone, thesis, or PhD, doctoral level, dissertation or thesis, sit down and have a personal conversation about what it was like when they got their degree, and what their personal expectations are of students and timing and feedback.
2. Go through the additional resources at the end of this chapter and use them appropriately. As examples, the American Psychological Association (APA, 2015) ethical stance on student rights has many points worthy of discussion, and the article that suggests student logs are a means to equalize the conversation is worth reading.
3. Establish with your supervisor as to what their role is – project manager or are you their apprentice? You can get a feel for this by asking, "From their perspective how independent do you need to be?" "When do they want you to come to them?" "When do they expect you to figure it out on your own?" "What are the key milestones you need to shoot for in your work?" "How will you know when you have completed a milestone?" "When you feel you need help or should ask a question, how quickly can you expect them to respond?"
4. Your foremost goal is to graduate, therefore you should work with your supervisor to complete a degree plan and establish a reasonable schedule of tasks for completion, if it is not required by your university to do so. After discussing the tenor of the

relationship, be sure to include the expected timing for key milestones.

Your goal is to build a collaborative relationship from the beginning when possible. Review the sections of this book on negotiation and managing people as you consider other steps.

Motivation

Even if you have the best relationship with your teachers, professors, mentors, and supervisors you may find that motivation comes and goes. Perhaps this is less likely to happen at the Masters' level where you mostly will finish in two years, but it certainly happens (probably a hundred percent of the time) at the doctoral level. Complex long-range tasks are difficult to maintain over the course of busy lives. You are required to add extra hours in an already busy day, to force your mind to focus on work that may feel like minutia when you are already tired, and to forgo pleasure in order to get your research and writing done. That motivation is difficult to maintain.

This is especially true when you don't know or have a pathway on which you are walking, but you feel like you're making it up as you go along. Symptoms of lack of motivation include procrastination, anxiety, depression, and of course regularly missing deadlines. Yet, even when faced with these symptoms, you may be tempted to look at pushing through towards the outcome, rather than dealing with the underlying challenge. The exercise that follows the next discussion helps you analyze, and then move forward towards positive motivation about your work.

A theoretical picture about personal growth or change. I have used this exercise so often that I have forgotten the psychological work that underpins it. The basic theoretical premise is that our past and our previous ways of doing things have greater influence the more we get away from them as we build new skills. Picture a room and you are crossing it. You are tethered to one wall with a large rubber band. As you progress towards the other wall the tension on that rubber band exerts itself more and more on your body until the time that you feel like you can go no further because of it holding you back. Picture also another rubber band that you have grabbed onto from the far side of the room (your future goal). It is exerting influence as well. Your challenge, when you have lost motivation, is to move into the sphere of influence of the band pulling you forward more than what is holding you back.

Exercise. Take a few moments and answer the following questions. Building a mind stage is a proven tool when you feel stuck.

1. What thoughts come to mind when you consider being successful? Are they thoughts that were developed in your childhood about your relative worthiness or skill level? Are they thoughts that indicate your fear of the goals you have chosen for yourself? Are they thoughts that in other ways make you feel small or less worthy?
2. Think about yourself at graduation, having achieved the goals that you thought of when you started, what can you say about your life? What opportunities do you have that were not possible before?
3. Now that you have established the two sides of the room from the previous analogy, focus for a moment on the thoughts and ideas that are coming from your past. An exercise from neuro-linguistic programming (NLP) will help you diminish their effect. Picture the thoughts that make you feel tethered and small. Make that picture grey in color. Now see them getting lighter, as though a fog rolled in. Then diminish their volume. Now see the rubber band around you that is tethered to those thoughts as beginning to disintegrate, getting smaller and smaller while at the same time the goal, the feeling of success, becomes brighter, more colorful, and stronger in your mind. See yourself, literally, on a stage pulling yourself forward towards that positive outcome. The positive outcomes get brighter, more vibrant and you feel the success in your heart as the other side grays out and diminishes.
4. Feel the positive change, imagine you have gotten to your goal. Make that picture big, bright and colorful and let your joy fill your body-mind experience. When you really have it, cement it by pinching your wrist (or some other noticeable action that can be repeated). Feel the success, pinch your wrist – over and over. When done with the intention to be able to recall those feelings,

this last step allows you to re- activate your body-mind memory of success whenever you need it.

This helpful mind stage can be used and developed over time. With just a few thoughts you put yourself on the stage, you imagine what's holding you back. You see yourself sticking to the back wall. You see yourself pulling forward but tension slowing you down. Then when you get halfway, you picture your goal. It is reaching out to you getting brighter and brighter as the past diminishes grace out and eventually loses its hold on you.

Re-engagement

As mentioned earlier in this book, a wise person told me once that it is not how well we do but how well we get back to doing when we stop that counts. There is no long-term goal that does not have starts and stops, challenges, or places where motivation completely dies. Sometimes the barriers are physical, as in running out of financial support. Or perhaps you have faced time and energy constraints, such as taking care of ill family members, having to navigate working promotions in the midst of graduate school, or perhaps getting sick yourself. Whatever the reason you may have disengaged, re-engaging is harder than being able to go step by step all the way through.

Trials do not make re-engaging impossible. Remember that for every challenge you are facing, others who have finished have faced it as well. It is also true that some have quit rather than finish. You are the one that decides whether or not you will push through to the end. If you are committed to graduation, then getting the proper help when you are faced with severe challenges is absolutely necessary.

Depending on how long a time out you have taken, you may be up against a time limitation imposed by your university policies. These, if you face them need to be negotiated first. The only thing that will keep you from stopping once you have disengaged, is not being aware of the timing or other legally based, challenges you face You do not want to proceed with your research, only to run into a policy where you can no longer enroll.

Exercise. Do you know how long your university gives you to finish? Your first step when facing the need to reengage is to seek guidance in your graduate school or program and have a serious conversation about where the challenges you have faced have put you on that timeline. Should you be in serious danger, because the work left is greater than the time allowed, your first effort must be to renegotiate your timeline and requirements so you are not working against all odds.

Assuming that the time allowed seems reasonable, the next step is to renegotiate the relationship with your committee and others you work with. By in large, academics want students to finish, and they are willing to work with those who have disengaged and want to come back. That does not mean that trust has not been lost, because likely it has. Most often when students lose motivation and disengage they fall into the trap of not meeting timelines, not delivering documents when they should, etc. From the other side of the desk this equates to not being trustworthy. It's important for any student working it re-engaging to come back to the people they will work with and have a serious conversation that reestablishes trust. Should you have those conversations and not feel at the outcome that your working relationships are back on track, your next step may be to work with your school or program to investigate a change in support personnel. At this juncture you have to steer your own ship – I have seen too many flounder when their instincts told them that a previous issue had become an insurmountable error to others and yet they tried to push ahead with bad relationships.

Once you've established that: a) you have a decent amount of time, b) you are working with people with whom you can negotiate both time and support, and c) you have overcome the challenges that caused the disengagement, then the last real negotiation needs to be between you and you.

Are you ready to be disciplined in your graduate work? You need to maintain habits, support structures, and continuous positive reinforcements that will help you keep your feet on the road to finishing. Those habits include 15 minutes a day minimum of constant work, Pomodoro timers to keep your focus high, outside guidance in the form of coaches or books, etc. It is likely that you will use all of these and more to help you set your own minor milestones and keep working on the tract that will get you finished.

How to finish a big task when your life is already full

Chances are that when you started your graduate work you might have had a little leeway in your life and you thought this would be the perfect time to get an advanced degree. As the work develops it usually becomes daunting. For non-traditional students, older, working, with family, children, older parents, etc. the challenge of layering graduate work onto an already full life can seem impossible. The ability to manage the stress and succeed is a key topic for a job interview as the discipline, resilience and time management required make you a prime candidate for further top-level tasks.

How then do people do it? You may say there are only so many hours in the day. If you are one of the many students whose life is full prior to graduate work then your final thesis or dissertation may seem an impossibility. Likely, you have tried to set hours aside, planned ahead, decided that you could get four hours done on Saturday, only to find that those hours diminish in their productivity or are interrupted by other demands.

I'm sure that for some people putting a little bit of time here in a little bit of time there works. It never worked for me. What does work for me, originally for my dissertation and later for the four books I have written, is adding an hour to an hour and a half every morning to my already busy life. I can't get more hours in the day, I can get less sleep. Rather than being disheartened because I'm not getting my big project done, I'm encouraged and motivated because I see the mountain of the big task chipped away, step-by-step.

All process starts with a good outline. The first step is that you have to know where you're going and believe your thought strategy will get you there. Under the resources tab you'll find links to the beginning your masters or your doctoral work with the end in mind, and these videos take you through the process of critically analyzing others work so that you can chart your own course. Refer to the section at the beginning on knowing why you are doing this as your goal will help your resilience when life seems overwhelming.

Exercise. This is how I take on big tasks and finish them while not interrupting the rest of my life (much) – try it and then modify for your needs.

The work prior to this is all design – what will you be saying and in what order? Once you have an outline of all your headings then the tools I use are Evernote, Microsoft Word, and Dragon software on my phone. Of course, there are other tools, these are the ones that work for me.

The process looks like this. The table of contents at the end will be drastically different than the one at the start. Your ideas and tone evolve as you write, and even more so as you revise, but this pathway gets you started.

- The outline of next tasks in order is transferred to a checklist in Evernote.
- Every morning at 5 AM-5:30 I come up to my desktop, open up that checklist and begin to write the next step on the list. Alternatively, if I've finished a rough draft, I proceed with an hour of revisions.
- I do most of my first writing using Dragon by Nuance. This software resides on my smartphone. I've used the evolving versions of Dragon for every book other than my dissertation, and the new phone version is by far the most accurate.
- I open up a new document every day in Dragon, and I start that document with the date and then the title as written on my checklist. These small habits help me avoid work going missing.
- I begin by writing/talking. I stop when I need to refer to outside sources on my desktop, restarting as necessary.
- When I finish that section, or an hour and a half has gone by, whichever comes first, I save what I have dictated to Evernote and sync. I now have two copies, one on my phone and one in Evernote on my computer.
- When I have finished an entire section, or chapter, I export it to Microsoft Word making sure that the headings which I have included in my dictation, become properly defined as Heading 1, Heading 2, etc. in word. Making sure I have the pane open, I can now double check against/the outline open in Evernote.
- The next steps are revision, revision, and more revision. As I have written I have captured my thoughts, next steps and doubts in a parking lot, on a white board. I refer to these as a checklist when I revise.

- Revisions proceed by first reading all of the dictated material and building the voice. Then I read and edit for consistency between sections and how things are laid out. Finally, readjusting sections to enhance flow and readability. At the end, just before peer review, Microsoft read aloud tool reads the entire document out loud and I edit everything that doesn't sound right to my ear..

To Consider as You Face Troubled Waters

We are all just people, more similar than different. People by and large enjoy helping each other and people at your university will be committed to helping you. Therefore, if you don't find the right support, or you are unsuccessful with negotiating what you need, keep going. Until you have knocked on every door, you have not done everything you can in your own behalf. Even if all the doors are shut there are ways to complain that can open them again. When the idea of telling people what you face makes you feel small, consider going first to people who make you feel good and then asking them to mediate or advocate for you. Graduate school should be tough, it should not diminish your human spirit.

Issues with Committees or Others You Depend On

If you are at your wits end, considering disengaging from your graduate work, likely it is another person who has caused the most trauma. At the root of the truly serious issues is a failure to communicate. An assumption then is if you (or the other person) had developed the skills previously discussed in this book you would have less likelihood of running into these challenges. However, it takes two people to develop a bad situation, and sometimes you are just stuck in a place where it appears almost nothing will work.

Academic Work Life is Not Easy

The human challenge is to constantly prove oneself intellectually, in an environment which is often contentious. Peer review, while an excellent tool for helping everyone have the best possible writing, research outcomes, etc. also sets up a mood of interaction which is constantly questioning. This is not helpful or useful to the human psyche on a day in and day out basis. Frequently people become guarded and develop barriers against the rest of the world, becoming less personally communicative rather than more forthcoming. Therefore, you may not be given all the information you need to navigate these waters.

Defensiveness takes on many modes. You and or your professors may be caught in a trap where one or both of you are defending against criticism by staying with what has worked in the past. A powerful defense inhibits flexible cognition. New ideas or ideas outside of that persons' context will be routinely denied, leading to a situation where others do not "feel heard."

Add on to this picture, a common challenge of difficulty communicating across demographic cohorts. The degree of change over the last decades is staggering, causing difficulty in the ability to keep up with the ways ideas are changing. Research methodologies as an example have burgeoned in the last two decades and few, if any, academics are aware of the leading edges on all of them.

The communication you care about is that which influences the relationship you have with those who ultimately have the power to ease or frustrate your graduation. This section looks at three specific challenges known to cause such frustration and offers reflective opportunities for anyone facing them to develop the tools or find the support that helps them overcome the challenge. The sections below include ambiguity, managing expectations, and dealing with either too much or too little independence. A failure to communicate is a complex issue, having at its heart two sets of human needs, ways of seeing the world and personal histories, all of which play their part in your current situation. Both the personal and the professional side of these lead to some suggestions as to ways you might want to proceed.

Ambiguity

The Cambridge advanced learner's dictionary and thesaurus defines ambiguity as the fact that something has more than one possible meaning and therefore may cause confusion. Language is complex, nuanced, and our personal backgrounds and cultural contexts inhibit our understanding exactly what another means with the words that they use. The particular context in cultures that cause confusion in graduate school are those of research backgrounds and personal history with education.

Let's take for example a student who has always had very good luck communicating with professors. Suddenly their experience changes when they begin to work with a highly respected person in their field, perhaps that person comes from a different culture as well. Communication begins to break down, the student begins to have a feeling of insecurity as they are significantly unprepared for the quicksand that words can cause when they don't comprehend the exact meaning or requirements.

The only way through ambiguity is to address it. The challenge with addressing ambiguity is that if it is not well done, in such a manner as the other person also understands the confusion the ambiguity has caused, they may become defensive. No one likes to be challenged, and academics least of all.

Good habits. I would strongly suggest that you never talk to a person who has ultimate control over your graduation without taking notes. What you want to capture in your notes is the exact language they use when they are directive. The reason for this is that when you run into a situation where meaning was not clear, you can go back to them telling them exactly what you heard them say and how you interpreted it. This allows them to point out the differences in that interpretation without becoming defensive. When you have a written record of previous conversations the following exercise becomes easier.

Exercise. PhD Comics has a picture for what Jorge Cham called the Aura of Distortion. I've linked it in additional resources, and it sets up the context for this exercise.

The following sentence stems are useful for you to employ as you finish a meeting with a supervisor. They will help you identify the nuanced portions of ambiguity that pertain to your particular situation. The outcome sought is that you will be able to express confusion without diminishing yourself or implying that the other person was not clear. Your goal is to understand.

1. I may be interpreting your words incorrectly. What I understand you to mean is that ...
2. May I come back to you with my partial response to your requests in order to avoid any misunderstanding? If so, can I...
3. In order to be efficient and clear can I just repeat back to you what I think is required here?
4. (to be used once some work is done and you run into difficulty) I seem to be running into difficulty, probably caused by my lack of understanding of exactly what you meant the last time we talked. May I take a moment just to express what is going on to help the process be efficient?

Managing Expectations

You have two sets of expectations you need to manage because unmet expectations cause trust to break down. You have to manage your own in that you don't set your expectations so high that you are discouraged either by your own performance or by the performance of people you work with. You also need to manage the expectations of those you work with, so that they do not lose trust in your performance. In both these cases, once trust is lost, it will color future interactions. In most situations, finishing all required work without further disappointment is the only way you will get it back.

Deadlines, timelines, calendars, and regular interactions or notes are all the tools of managing expectations. But so is sensitive awareness during conversation. It is useful rather than harmful to pick up the clues given by someone's facial expression, and to come back to them saying, "I may be reading something into this, but I noticed an expression on your face that made me wonder if...."

The ability to openly discuss feelings as well as ideas may not be common in your life or that of the people you work with. This is especially possible if and when people are coming from different cultures or fields of study. Therefore, it is your responsibility to be openly aware, and to communicate past any negative potential that you sense. If this is not possible or if you see the relationship deteriorating in any way, call for help, by discussing the situation with another trusted ally, sooner rather than later, and plot a different course of action. More about this at the end of this section.

Your university also has expectations of both you and your professors behavior. Be on firm ground. Go to and look up guidelines for students, and any documentation about communication with professors, provided by your university. Have a conversation with advisors, about student and professors requirements and ask them for any documentation they are aware of. It is far better to surface these with a half an hour's inquiry before you begin to craft the relationship that will help you graduate.

Exercise. The basic exercise to manage expectations is: a) have a conversation, b) agree upon deadlines and requirements, c) write them down and share them in written form with all parties impacted by those decisions, d) stay in touch without taking up time such with an email one week prior to delivering any required documents. These notices basically tell the other you are delivering on time and say, "I'm going to make our agreed-upon deadline and you will have the X, Y, and Z said by…"

More words do not necessarily produce better meaning. This is especially true when you are being completely open and authentic while scared. Since graduate work has a strong power differential between professors and students it is not uncommon for fear to come into that equation. I strongly recommend that when you are writing to anyone who has ultimate power over your final work that you write it, walk away, come back and edit out all unnecessary language and any emotional intonations. Look at written communication with these powerful people in your life as you would a neutral business situation where you and someone else were building something together. How would you discuss a building project with the contractor? That might be a tonality to your words which will prove helpful.

Too Much or Too Little Independence

Gardner, S (2009) includes independence as one of the five frustrations that cause disengagement in graduate school. This may seem odd until one takes into account the purpose being to develop humanity to the

Masters and or Doctoral level, both of which require independent action. I think most academics would agree that as a student progresses through their masters and into their doctoral work they should be increasingly independent in their thought, and their ability to solve problems, and in their final outputs. However, depending upon the personal background of the professors you are dealing with, the actual level of independence may vary from, "Do it all yourself I never want to see your work until it's picture-perfect," to the opposite, "There is only one way to do this and I expect a, b, and c.". These two desperate positions may come up against equally disparate potential in students ranging from, "Get out of my way I know what I'm doing I have a clear idea." To, "I expect you to hold my hand and guide me through the process like every other educational experience I've had before now." Even more frustrating is that on any one continuum, circumstances may cause the person to flip to the other stance. The 2 x 2 chart below outlines the potential for disagreement based upon these two modes of thought. Of course, most people fall in the middle, and there is good and bad on both sides as you will see below. A solid strategy is to guide your behaviour, and to help your professors guide theirs, down a middle range.

	Professor – Do it my way or the highway	Professor: Be completely independent – shine without any help
Student – Your job is to guide my steps and ensure I am successful.	These two can build a bond that seems ideal to others, much like the student sitting at the feet of the expert in Raphael's Scholars of Athens. Breakdown may occur after graduation if the student did not develop necessary critical thought and analysis.	This is a tug of war. The students' choice is to become stronger (often by finding outside help) or to disengage from the relationship as the professor will like be an immovable wall in this regard.

Student – Get out of my way, I am coming through	This is either a fight or a spaceship, depending on the level of agreement between them. Should there be little agreement the two are likely to find no satisfaction from the relationship. Should they agree, however, the student has an ally who has greater experience going just where they want to go and will shine for very little time or emotional cost on the professors' part.	Works best when a student has a firm background in both the topic and the methodology. May cause absolute breakdown at final defense, if more guidance was needed

Figure 2: Matrix of potential graduate mentoring relationships based on level of independence

Calling for Help

As mentioned above, graduate work requires greater amounts of independence. That does not mean you should not ask for help when you are out of your depth. It does suggest however that you may choose to seek out that help from sources outside of the realm of the particular relationships that are causing the distress. In most human interactions when we suspect something is going on that we can't quite work out, we tend to go to friends or family members who may have insights prior to tackling the challenge head on. Within the graduate environment there are similarities.

What help is available on your campus differs from campus to campus, so do the responsibilities of the people who have been tasked with providing support to students. Therefore a good question to ask people is who here is responsible for student support? Generally, there are advisors, counselors, health and wellness practitioners, your graduate office, the registrar's office, etc. All of these, if not responsible for student support, will have a good idea of who is.

You don't have to share the challenge you're up against in order to ask to speak to someone who may be able to help. Depending on the political environment, you may want to simply inquire as to who is responsible for student support if a student is facing challenges with…

(insert a general classification). Should people begin to question you precisely, just say you would prefer to speak to only one person and who is the person or role they would recommend?

I can't say enough about getting help sooner rather than later. Having worked with students who paid years, literally years, of extra tuition because they were in a situation where those responsible for helping them graduate had lost faith in their ability to do so, the quicker you turn around a personal situation the better.

It's important not to feel small and helpless and give up. There are steps you can take. From asking for help, voicing a complaint, to officially complaining, each offers new potential. Depending on the situation you face, anyone employed by a university is held to certain standards, and whenever those standards are not met, you have a case worthy of putting in front of others. It all goes back to managing expectations, yours as well as theirs. You may have had unrealistic expectations, even expectations outside of the working norms of the University. Far better for you do be disabused of these then proceed for years thinking the problem is on their side. Take the time to find the neutral party who can help you figure out what university policies may be involved. Then you are in a position to make decisions about your next steps.

Timing Issues

Above all else, watch the clock. Remember, sooner is better than later. Every sticky situation will take time to correct, and time is not on your side. For one thing, you want to graduate. For another, your university has policies regarding the amount of time they can be held responsible to give you support. Once you start to push for resolution to a challenge that is holding you back, keep a calendar and mark down each interaction you have with university personnel. Should you need it, these records can be used to build a case to extend your time on the clock.

Additional Resources

- **Phd Comics Aura of Distortion:**
  http://phdcomics.com/comics/archive.php?comicid=1518

- **Managing your independence and skill development for academics and as job prep:** https://pd.education/job-prep-video-snippets/video/143-managing-your-independence-and-skill-development-for-academics-and-as-job-prep.html
- **Finding and Utilizing the Supports You Need in Graduate School:** https://pd.education/wellness-video-snippets/video/107-finding-and-utilizing-the-supports-you-need-in-graduate-school.html
- **Ending the Frustrations of Graduate School:** https://pd.education/wellness-video-snippets/video/142-ending-the-frustrations-of-graduate-school.html

Low Tide in Graduate Life

Three topics are covered in this section, with the caveat that it is not my intention to cover the specifics in detail. Rather, here you will find a brief discussion that each is serious and, should you be facing any of them, to offer ideas about who on campus can help. Included here are challenges that deans talk about regarding students (over) working in labs, challenges with food or other financial types of insecurity, and worry, anxiety, and imposter syndrome.

In the Lab

The first time I heard about challenges of students in a laboratory was when I had given a speech on preparing for the Viva, or final defense, to one of our member universities. Afterwards, a student came up to me with a great deal of anxiety, worried that she had given three years of her life to a situation and did not have the support she needed to finish. The situation, as I came to understand it, was that she had taken a fully supported PhD on a topic regarding cell mutation in biology from a researcher who was building his own career. He was constantly out of the lab, having conversations with funders, grant philanthropists, etc. and sponsored only the best and the brightest students to get the actual work done. Perhaps (and probably this had been his personal journey) he assumed that everyone who worked for him had, or would figure out, what was needed to complete the thesis and graduate. He did not, nor

114

had he anticipated, he would be asked to provide support for helping her gain the logic she needed to craft the thesis argument and pass final defense or Viva. The student I was talking to had no comprehension of the challenges of writing up research that she had not designed, and making it a coherent case across a standard five chapter dissertation or thesis. She felt she was being treated as though she was stupid to even be asking him about these issues.

Deans discuss a second type of challenge pertaining to bad situations in labs. Some professors whose grants fully support international students, may consider graduate students in the same light they would a paid research assistant under other more industrial circumstances. In other words, the researcher, who wrote the grant, and brings in the money that supports the student tuitions, is interested in getting as much work, and quality laboratory time, out of graduate students as is possible. This can result in completely egregious work situations for the students, with some being expected to put in 60 or 70 hour work weeks, with expectations to sleep in the lab if necessary to monitor the research, etc.

The relationship between you as a graduate student and the person who is supporting your research is contractual. You have the right to negotiate the working relationship and I recommend you see also the next section with the APA rights documentation. Discussions are best handled before you start the work. However, if you, or someone you know, is in jeopardy there are many on campus who will want to mediate a better situation. Inquire in the graduate office about who on your campus takes care of issues that have to do with contractual agreements between students in lab and their supporting research supervisors. Someone will mediate the issue for you.

Food or Housing Insecurity

It is not uncommon, that you may face difficulty making ends meet, paying the rent, finding food to put on the table, or face a situation where paying for other life necessities becomes difficult. While from the universities perspective you could be fully supported, if you travel from another country, have a family, etc., graduate stipends and assistantships are not usually at the level where these extra requirements are easily covered.

115

Early in the evolution of DoctoralNet as a business, we were contacted by a master student in business who wanted an internship with us. It became clear that this student, an international student from India, was living at the very edge of possible existence. His clothes were thin, as appropriate for his country, but not appropriate for winter in Ireland. He had a room that he was sharing with other people, and finding places to study was difficult. And probably he ate more Ramen noodles than was healthy.

Depending on where you are in the world, different supports for basic food and shelter may be available to you. We have heard of many creative outlets. These range from your engaging in part-time or freelance work opportunities to searching out the support systems in the community around the University that offer food to poor, transient, or homeless people. Opportunities on campus are also developing, so investigate if yours has a food or clothing bank.

Reaching out before you are desperate is the key. There is no harm or shame involved in going into your graduate office and saying it is difficult to make ends meet, with food and shelter becoming an issue, and what supports do they know of that you should pursue?

Worry, Anxiety, and Imposter Syndrome

Only you can analyze and decide where you are on the continuum from worry through anxiety and where your discomfort may lay. Every human being has at one time or another wrestled with thoughts and feelings that inhibit their free motion or sense of security. That does not mean that it is just your fate if you are faced with a regular inability to sit down and proceed with your work because of clenching feelings in your solar plexus or major headaches. If you are worried about the outcome of the situation to the extent it is making you feel ill, you should reach out and take action to alleviate your pain.

Everyone worries. But when worrying thoughts cannot be turned off or inhibit work, or if worry gets you up in the middle of the night and you have trouble sleeping, then you are entering into concerns that are more properly called anxiety. Anxiety escalates, is frequently triggered by situations which are common to your life and may completely immobilize you for periods of time. It is not uncommon in graduate school.

You should know the symptoms. If your worry does not go away on its own or gets worse over time you should seek help. Campuses have doctors, and mental health providers, and seeing them before your anxiety gets worse will help you get rid of it faster. There are many nonmedical interventions. They include religious practice, student groups. anxiety clinics, meditation, yoga, etc. Test out nonmedical interventions first because medicines may dull your sense of self and brain function. (*Mayo Clinic, 2019*).

Exercise. Let yourself off the hook.

Take a moment and write down all the commitments you are responsible for. Make this a four-column chart with the left column listing the commitment. Column B is the amount of time per week (or month) it takes. Column C is who you are responsible to. Finally, column D is whether or not it is absolutely mandatory that YOU do the work.

Next, go back and highlight the ones that are totally your responsibility. How much time is left for graduate school? Taken together, do they add up to more hours than you have? If so, you are overcommitted, and something will need to change. If close to the limit but doable by themselves, then begin to question who can help you with the ones that are a lesser priority or for which you can ask support from others.

You should have a clear plan, calendar or other system where you keep your task requirements out in front of you. Rather than being a pressure, this list actually alleviates anxiety for most people. Just the ability to write it down, and compartmentalize it, should give you some distance so that you can focus on your immediate work.

In my own office (as I have mentioned previously), I have a small whiteboard propped up in front of my printer. I write down tasks as they come up and sometimes it is difficult to find space on the board. Yet, there is a huge amount of satisfaction in cleaning them off when I complete them. I've learned that the general crowdedness of the board grows and diminishes over time. This allows me to keep the things which may cause later challenges up in front of me. Even when I am not addressing them, knowing they are not forgotten, satisfies my unconscious self, diminishing the fear that I will forget something. Do I have flashes of, "Oh, there is too much here, I will never get done"? Of course, but I can keep those to quick thoughts and then get back to the work of completing the next task so I can wipe it off the slate.

Imposter syndrome. Research on imposter syndrome has developed over the years as it became clear that many people in high leadership positions privately agreed that they have in the back of their head a voice that doubts their accomplishments or they have a persistent internalize fear of being exposed as a fraud. Young (2011) divided these issues into five types: the perfectionist the superwoman/man, the natural genius, the soloist and the expert. The perfectionist set excessively high goals and then when they don't reach one they trounce themselves (and others) with (self)-doubt. The superwoman/man are convinced they are phonies in the midst of people who are the real deal, so they have to put in extra hours and deny themselves a personal life or down time. The natural genius fits well with Carol Dweck's fixed mindset (2015). If this is you, you judge your competence at a new task by how easy it is. If you have to work hard, you experience shame or a sense of not being good enough. The soloist never asks for help as that is also shameful. If you are an "expert" by Young's model, then you base your competence by what and how much you know, which of course, is a set-up for feelings of failure in a world with never-ending amounts of knowledge available.

If one or more of these sounds like you, then know that self-awareness, meditation, and other techniques aimed to ease internal stress, will be useful. It all starts with understanding that you are not alone and that others have faced these situations and been able to make them diminish so that that voice has little or no effect on their lives over time. No one should live with constant feelings of not being good enough, so seek help/support if you need it. Sharing your feelings with others is a start. You'll find you are not alone.

Genetic Components of Stress

This section was called low tide in graduate life because, like the tides, these situations vary in intensity and are episodic. Everyone may encounter some if not all of these in their graduate careers. Whether they cause long-term and harmful effects though has a great deal of variation. For some they will engender helplessness and hopelessness and victim responses for life. For others, these troubles or insecurities may bring up feelings of resentment or depression. Still others may face a full-fledged identity crisis and find themselves wanting to throw it all in and start a new life. Be aware that some of these responses and outcomes may have genetic components. Therefore, should you see yourself on a track that is getting worse you might want to investigate whether and how others in your family have experienced similar levels of difficulty. Lessons have been learned, some solutions worked, and others caused more distress. It should not be surprising that the memories of the older generation might be able to help you find the solutions you look for. At the least, you'll find the relief that comes with knowing you are not alone.

Research into physiologically stressful situations show that stress reduces working memory and therefore has a negative effect on cognitive functioning. In lab tests, two effects stand out - feelings of pressure and a drop off in accuracy (which of course increases pressure). The following exercise developed out of this research and has been shown to "eliminate poor performance" in the laboratory (*Beilock, 2011*).

Exercise. Feeling stressful and having trouble getting to work? Take 10 minutes and write your thoughts and feelings in a journal. Pour out every thought you don't want to acknowledge so you can let them go prior to starting the day. Remember Beilock's team found just 10 minutes of writing could eliminate poor performance. The greater the pressure the greater the relief as your body-mind can relax.

Work-life Challenges

It's not uncommon for graduate students to have added work-life issues such as taking care of aging parents or sick children. Or for you to go through personal challenges, including but not limited to divorce, job change, moving, etc. Managing work-life can lead to areas of such distress that other challenges in this section are heightened.

Options to Consider. The following are what others have done before you that has worked. This is not an exercise, but rather a list of optional ideas that will be cumulative over time, relieving your stress.

1. Tell your colleagues about your obligations when you have difficulty managing both family and academics.
2. Be willing to say "No" to extra work and job duties when your outside obligations begin to take up more time. Managing academics and the rest of your life is difficult. People will understand when you say no when you must. Do not take on more than you can hold.
3. See what you can do to ease the burdens of your work life obligations. This could be giving yourself time for a movie, so you relax, or simply deciding not to complete a non-necessary task. Both allow you moments of control.
4. Set a calendar and stick to it. As mentioned before, writing (or approaching any of the big tasks on your plate) for just 15 minutes a day will keep you moving ahead when times are tough.
5. Take care of yourself. You've chosen a goal that is demanding and not always compatible with intense family demands and obligations. If there is a time when you can't do both, negotiate around it with your graduate school. It is not a sign of weakness that you know how to manage yourself well enough to redo obligations when necessary.

Additional Resources

- **Worry, Anxiety, Imposters syndrome - what are they, what can you do?- WORKSHEET:** https://pd.education/file-downloads/wellness/372-worry-anxiety-imposters-syndrome-what-are-they-what-can-you-do-worksheet-20190408.html
- **Working or Parenting Students Survival Guide PDF:** https://pd.education/file-downloads/academic-hacks-tools/150-working-or-parenting-students-survival-guide-pdf-22-feb-16.html
- **Moving Towards Independent Work and Finishing for ABDs and Masters:** https://pd.education/file-downloads/thesis-design/517-20200729-moving-towards-independent-work-and-finishing-for-abds-and-masters.html
- **How to Increase Your Work Life Grad Balance and Decrease Your Anxiety SLIDES:** https://pd.education/file-

downloads/wellness/456-how-to-increase-your-work-life-grad-balance-and-decrease-your-anxiety-slides-20191125-group.html
- **Positive Psychology Helping Attitude and Work Life Balance:** https://pd.education/wellness-video-snippets/video/109-positive-psychology-helping-attitude-and-work-life-balance.html

Your Rights: Legal and Ethical

While ethics are the same throughout academia, the legal considerations and policies under which your university performs its duties will be different depending on where you live. If you are a student in the United States, as an example, the rules your graduate school adheres to will be different state to state and whether your university is public or private. The final document required by masters and doctoral students around the world vary widely. Because of these factors. anything in this section should be taken as a generality only. From here you must investigate further at your local level.

The challenges to student rights need not be big, contentious, litigation producing issues. Rather, they include simple questions. Examples include whether or not you were given all the necessary information about your financial support issues, whether communication was done in a timely fashion, and whether you were treated in a respectful manner (APA, 2015). Questions of ethical and legal guidelines are presented here as a means for you to judge the spectrum of possibilities that you have actually experienced, and to give you guidelines and methods where you can question what is going on around you without having to veer into being contentious.

Far better for you to be able to bring in the APA guidelines, as an example, and say, "I understand these exist and am wondering to what extent, and how, we can move forward to best match this experience?" As the APA itself says, "as a graduate student knowing your rights will not alleviate all of the fears associated with speaking up, but it can help you with the critical first step: starting the conversation" (Cummings, 2016). This might include sending a copy of these rights to your department, chair, or advisor. You might try using language such as, " I'd like to discuss right 3.6 with you in regards to…" as a way to initiate dialogue. By referring to explicitly stated rights you can focus the discussion on standards for respect and responsibilities rather than on anecdotal claims. The position statement can also provide you with the confidence of knowing that there are others who are passionate about protecting the rights of graduate students.

Finally, prior to going into a general discussion of those ethical standards, I just want to say that your graduate Dean is on the side of protecting your rights. If you feel that any situation in which you are involved egregiously flies in the face of any of the things listed in the APA standards, then by all means, go see the people in your graduate school about the situation. It is a shame, when as I heard at a Council of Graduate Schools meeting, the Dean states that a student had taken a situation all the way to litigation, before she even heard it existed. Much better to get these situations sorted out early rather than late. If you want someone to anonymously address an issue with your department you have to go to the graduate school first. Once you've gone to your program, that is a smaller population and they will know who is being represented later.

Ethical Standards for Academic Relationships with Students

How a graduate student should be treated (especially psychology students as that is their purview), or the expectations they should be able to have of their university have been most carefully drawn out by the APA. The full document is listed with the URL to access it in the reference list.

Ethical standards include...

1. A respectful institutional environment that assures the health and well-being of students
2. Policies from the University that allow for open dialogue when situations are not conducive to personal and professional growth
3. Professional and educational training opportunities which include quality interactions with Professorial staff, other varied social and programmatic opportunities, and robust professional development aimed at a well-rounded and successful graduate career.

4. A work environment that has fair compensation, an ability to study in a situation free of exploitation, and safety, free from harassment.
5. Policies that allow for respectful and open appeals and grievances without negative consequences brought on as a result.

These rights and ethical standards are backed up by a position statement on the need for consistent mentoring and training in doctoral programs and is also available from the American Psychological Association.

Legal Rights

Delving into legal rights is a much murkier discussion because the context of the situation, the particular local environment, etc. will of course be different in every situation. That said, a few comments about proposals and contracts in a overarching legal sense may have bearing, as information from other authors may allow you to consider your situation.

As with all things legal, hard evidence is needed. Both sides will argue about whether or not the institution or its agents failed (as examples) to provide accommodations for disability, violated procedural or substantive due process rights, discriminated against the student, or breached in its contractual obligations. Therefore, a first step in considering whether or not you have a case worthy of further discussion is to pull together all the evidentiary information you have. Emails, calendar notes, journal writing, etc. provide non-emotional points of reference. You may be living in a situation that you find difficult, but others will have a different view. Therefore, be careful to have evidence, and not emotion.

Is a university legally contracted to give you a graduate diploma? No. The educational system has rigorous guidelines and expectations, and work must be to those standards. However, in the United States, there are some protections, again differing state to state. If you have written and defended a three chapter proposal prior to gathering doctoral research, then in some instances that proposal has been seen as a legally binding document that protects the student from facing egregious change being required later by their committees. In other words, your advisor or mentor, should they leave, cannot be replaced by someone who wants you to do something entirely different.

Many universities have well-established and fully posted student Bill of Rights. A first step then is to go look to see what is published in terms of guidelines for students, Bill of Rights for students, complaints for students, etc. on your university website.

In the United Kingdom, the state provides an ombudsman who will look into grievances between universities and students, only after the complaint process at the University has been tried and no mediation was possible. The fact of the ombudsman potential, often encourages the University to have people who are excellent at mediating between two positions available to step in, listen to both sides, and help the student proceed, I worked closely with the student to had a mediator assigned as part of a complaint, and while the road to graduation still took an additional year and a half, he was able to move past the never ending cycle of revisions without full disclosure or discussion. The road to complaint is not easy, but neither is living with or trying to work through a situation that seems doomed to failure.

The earlier you begin negotiations, because you feel in your heart that a situation you are facing is not fair or will not lead to graduation, the better. While every institution hopes that all faculty will be open, respectful, and willing to guide students through to success, personalities and opinions come into these challenges. Sometimes the mix between you and your supervisor or mentor is just not a good one. Rather than continue in a situation that feels ambiguous, or disrespectful, it is best to speak up, ask questions, and see whether shifts can be made, or situations can be handled differently.

In Conclusion

This chapter dealt with the unfortunate side of graduate work. While a relatively small population of students will experience the kinds of challenges discussed here, all students should understand their rights, and responsibilities. I close by saying that while we always wish anyone in graduate life only the best, I also hope you have an awareness of yourself and are guiding your own ship through these waters.

You can learn from all the human interactions on campus, and they can set you up for a more positive work environment throughout the rest of your life. If you are embroiled in any of the troubled waters discussed here, it may be difficult to see the "light at the end of the tunnel" but it does exist. Everything is a learning situation that will stand you in good stead later.

I hope that this short volume has given you a perspective or point of view that will allow you to guide your ship more safely to the safe harbor of graduation and onto the rest of your career. With that, and with great respect, I close

E. Alana James, Ed.D

References

Adevey, G., (2013). *The leader in you: realizing your leadership qualities for greatness.* iUniverse.

APA. (2015). *APAGS Position Statement on the Rights of Psychology Graduate Students.* Retrieved from https://www.apa.org/apags/issues/student-rights-position

Beilock, S. (2011, 26 August). *Back to school: dealing with academic stress.* Psychological Science Agenda, Sept 2011. https://www.apa.org/science/about/psa/2011/09/academic-stress

Csikszentmihalyi, M. (2020). *Finding flow: The psychology of engagement with everyday life.* Basic Books.

Covey, S. R. (1989). *The seven habits of highly effective people: restoring the character ethic.* Simon and Schuster.

Covey, S. R. (2003). *The 7 habits of highly effective people personal workbook.* Simon & Schuster.

Covey, S. R. (2016). *The seven habits of highly successful people: 25th anniversary edition.* Rosetta Books.

Cummings, J. (July 2016). *Knowing your graduate rights.* Retrieved May 9, 2020 from https://www.apa.org/science/about/psa/2016/07/graduate-student-rights

Din, E.. (2010). *Find yourself in the service of other.* Phi Delta Kappan; Vol. 91, Iss. 5, (Feb 2010): 35-36.

Dorner, D. (1996). *The logic of failure: Recognizing and avoiding error in complex situations.* Perseus Books.

Duckworth, A. L., Peterson, C., Matthews, M. D., & Kelly, D. R. (2007). *Grit: Perseverance and passion for long-term goals. Journal of Personality and Social Psychology,* 92(6), 1087–1101. https://doi.org/10.1037/0022-3514.92.6.1087

Durfee, E. H. (1999). *Practically Coordinating.* AI Magazine, 20(1), 99. https://doi.org/10.1609/aimag.v20i1.1443

Dutton, J.E., Ragins, B. R. (2007). *Exploring positive relationships at work: Building a theoretical and research foundation.* Lawrence Erlbaum Associates

Dweck, C. (2015). *Carol Dweck revisits the growth mindset.* Education Week, 35(5), 20-24.

Dweck, C. S., & Yeager, D. S. (2019). *Mindsets: A View From Two Eras.* Perspectives on Psychological Science, 14(3), 481–496. https://doi.org/10.1177/1745691618804166

Fave A.D., Brdar I., Vella-Brodrick D., Wissing M.P. (2013) *Religion, Spirituality, and Well-Being Across Nations: The Eudaemonic and Hedonic Happiness Investigation.* In: Knoop H., Delle Fave A. (eds) Well-Being and Cultures. Cross-Cultural Advancements in Positive Psychology, vol 3. Springer

Gabrys, R.L., Tabir, N., Anisman,H., and Matheson, K. (2018). *Cognitive Control and Flexibility in the Context of Stress and Depressive Symptoms: The Cognitive Control and Flexibility Questionnaire,* Frontiers of Psychology, 19 November 2018. https://doi.org/10.3389/fpsyg.2018.02219

Gardner, H. (2006). *Multiple intelligences: New horizons* (Completely rev. and updated. ed.).Basic Books.

Gardner, S. K. (2009). *Student and faculty attributions of attrition in high and low-completing doctoral programs in the United States.* Higher Education (58), 97-112.

Goleman, D. (1996). *Emotional intelligence.* Bantam Books.

Goleman, D., Boyatzis, R. E., & McKee, A. (2017). *Primal leadership: unleashing the power of emotional intelligence* (Tenth anniversary edition. ed.). Harvard Business Review Press.

Hogan, J., Hogan, R., and Busch, C. *"How to Measure Service Orientation"* Journal of Applied Psychology (69:1), 1984, pp. 167-173.

Holdaway, E.A., Debloise, C., and Winchester, I., (1995). *Supervision of graduate students.* Canadian Journal of Higher Education. 25(3), 1-29.

Hong, L., Page, S., (2004). *Groups of diverse problem solvers can outperform groups of high-ability problem solvers.* PNAS, November 16, 2004,

101, 46, 16385–16389.
www.pnas.org/cgi/doi/10.1073/pnas.0403723101

Mayo Clinic, (2019). *Generalized anxiety disorder.* Retrieved from
https://www.mayoclinic.org/diseases-conditions/generalized-anxiety-
disorder/diagnosis-treatment/drc-20361045

Marmot, M., Brunner, E., (2005) *Cohort Profile: The Whitehall II
study.* International Journal of Epidemiology, 34, 2, April 2005, Pages
251–256, https://doi.org/10.1093/ije/dyh372

McQueen, A. C. (2004). *Emotional intelligence in nursing work.*
Journal of advanced nursing, 47(1), 101-108.

Rittel, H. W., & Webber, M. M. (1973). *"Dilemmas in a General
Theory of Planning."* Policy sciences, 4(2), 155-169.
https://www.cc.gatech.edu/fac/ellendo/rittel/rittel-dilemma.pdf

Rubin R. D., Brown-Schmidt S., Duff M. C., Tranel D., Cohen
N. J. (2011). *How do I remember that I know you know that I know?* Psychol.
Sci. 22, 1574–1582 10.1177/0956797611418245

Schwab, K. (2016). *The fourth industrial revolution* (First U.S.
edition. ed.). Crown

Schwab, K., & Davis, N. (2018). *Shaping the future of the fourth
industrial revolution : a guide to building a better world* (First American edition.
ed.). Currency Business.

Seligman, M. E. P. (2011). *Flourish : a visionary new understanding of
happiness and well-being* (1st Free Press hardcover ed.). Free Press.

Stets and Burke 2014 (chapter 1)

World Economic Forum. (January 2016). *The future of jobs:
employment, skills and workforce strategy for the fourth industrial revolution.*
Retrieved from
http://www3.weforum.org/docs/WEF_Future_of_Jobs.pdf

Young, V. (2011). *The secret thoughts of successful women: Why capable
people suffer from the impostor syndrome and how to thrive in spite of it.* Crown.

Zahidi, S. (2020). *We need a global reskilling revolution – here's why.*
Retrieved from https://www.weforum.org/agenda/2020/01/reskilling-
revolution-jobs-future-skills/

129

Zamanzadeh, V., Jasemi, M., Valizadeh, L., Keogh, B., and Taleghani, F., (2015). *Effective factors in providing holistic care: a qualitative study.* IIndian J Palliat Care. 2015 May-Aug; 21(2): 214–224. doi: 10.4103/0973-1075.156506. Retrieved 5/9/202 from https://www.ncbi.nlm.nih.gov/pmc/articles/PMC4441185/

Index

Academic Writing 16–17

    Writing with Passion 47–48

Ambiguity ..... *See* Frustrations

Anxiety .... *See* Worry, Anxiety, and Imposter Syndrome

Argumentation 17–21

Bias 30–31

Body mind 2, 5, 51, 52, 53, 55, 59, 64, 101, 119

Cognitive Skills 33

Committee 106–13

Complex Problem Solving 38–39

Coordinating with others. 81–84

Creativity 34

Defending Your Ideas .. 28–29

Difficult people ...... *See* people management

Discipline 61–64

Ethical Standards 122–23

Eudaemonic well-being 52

Exercise

    Alleviate anxiety 117

    Alleviate anxiety 2 119

    Backwards mapping 9

Bias 31

Build consciousness 67

Building connections 71

Complex problem solving 38

Critical thinking 40

Discipline 63

Emotional intelligence ... 75

Flexible cognition 36

Focus 66

For anyone having trouble passing proposal 27

Getting unstuck 101

Habits 65

Investigate fallacies 23

Judgement and decision-making 42

Know your limits 102

Manage expectations 110

Meeting with supervisor 108

Mindset 56

Negotiating with supervisor or chair 83

Negotiation strategy 79

Negotions with committee or supervisor 99

People management 87

Prepare for negotiation ..78

Process for investigating new literature 15

Process to get the work done 104

Self-awareness 57

Start the research design process.............................26

Start with the end in mind 8

Style, emphasis, structure 47

Taking risks.....................70

Tighten it up 68

Time management matrix 7

To test the coherance of your research 29

Transferring ideas 69

Work-life balance 119

Fallacies...........................21–24

Flexible Cognition......... 35–37

Food or Housing Insecurity 115–16

Frustrations

    ambiguity............................2

    lack of support..................4

    skill development..............3

    too much or too little independence....................3

    work-life balance 2

Frustrations................... xvii, 88

Habits 64–71, 108–9

Identity 5–6

Imposter Syndrome............*See* Worry, Anxiety, and Imposter Syndrome

Independence......110–13, See Frustrations

Intelligence 33

Lab 114–15

Lack of Support ....See Frustrations

Legal Rights.................123–25

Metacognition ....55–58, See Also Motivation, See Also Body mind, See Also Routine, See Also Discipline, See Also Habits

Mind Body Spirit Connection 52–54

Mindset ..5, 51, 55, 56, 58, 97, 118, 128

Motivation 1, 100–102

People management 84–89

Personal Growth................ 5–6

Reading...........................12–15

Re-engagement 102–3

Research Design Logic 24

Resourcefulness 72–73

Routine.....................58–59, 60

Service Orientation.......90–91

Skill development ....See Frustrations

Software 60

Support......... See Frustrations

Thrive 51–52

Time management.............. 59

    Pomodoro technique 59

Time Management................ 9

Time management matrix.... 7

Transferrable Attitudinal Skills 73–74

Work-life balance .... See Frustrations

Work-Life Balance 104–6

Work-life Challenges . 119–20

CPSIA information can be obtained
at www.ICGtesting.com
Printed in the USA
LVHW021820261022
731637LV00005B/354

9 798582 294665